Help for the Evangelistic Preacher

Help for the EVANGELISTIC PREACHER

James E. Carter

BROADMAN PRESS
Nashville, Tennessee

Unless otherwise indicated, all Scripture quotations are from the King James Version of the Bible. Scripture quotations marked ASV are from the American Standard Version of the Bible. Scripture quotations marked Williams are from *The New Testament, a Translation in the Language of the People* by Charles B. Williams. Copyright 1937 and 1966. Moody Press, Moody Bible Institute of Chicago. Used by permission. Scripture quotations marked RSV are from the Revised Standard Version of the Bible, copyrighted 1946, 1952, © 1971, 1973. Scripture quotations marked GNB are from the *Good News Bible,* the Bible in Today's English Version. Old Testament: Copyright © American Bible Society 1976; New Testament: Copyright © American Bible Society 1966, 1971, 1976. Used by permission.

Library of Congress Cataloging in Publication Data

Carter, James E., 1935-
  Help for the evangelistic preacher.

  1. Evangelistic sermons. 2. Sermons, Americans.
3. Baptists—Sermons. 4. Sermons—Outlines, syllabi,
etc. I. Title.
BV3797.C249H45 1985   252'.3   83-70371
ISBN 0-8054-6243-0

Dedicated to the memory of Ira H. Peak, Sr.
who baptized me . . .
under whom I surrendered to the ministry . . .
and whose life and ministry centered on evangelism . . .
even unto death

41088

The Library
INTERNATIONAL CHRISTIAN
GRADUATE UNIVERSITY

CONTENTS

Part III . . .
Some Evangelistic Sayings

Preface

To preach evangelistically, in such a way that persons are brought to conviction and to the commitment of their lives in faith to Jesus Christ, is the continuing challenge of the Christian preacher. The note of the evangel must always be sounded clearly and convincingly as the Word of God is expounded and applied. The message must be biblically accurate, theologically correct, and personally applied at the same time.

In the heavy demands upon the preacher the resources for presenting the gospel and illustrating it often begin to run thin. The commitment to evangelistic preaching is there, the need to present the claims of Christ is evident, the desire to preach evangelistically is present, but the demands upon the resources at hand sometimes drain them away. How can one find a different way to present the gospel? Where can one find an illustration for that idea? What can spark the imagination to ignite the creative juices to produce another sermon?

This book is a resource book for the preacher who preaches evangelistic sermons. As in my earlier resource book on stewardship, *A Sourcebook for Stewardship Sermons* (Broadman), it is divided into three parts: some evangelistic sermons, some evangelistic stories, some evangelistic sayings. The sermons are my composition. The stories and sayings come from many sources, all of which are noted for your convenience. Some of them come from material I have written at other times. The uncredited entries are from articles I have written, usually in the church paper of the First Baptist Church, Natchitoches, Louisiana, or the University Baptist Church, Fort Worth, Texas—or both. The difference between stories and sayings may sometimes be in length, in nature, or in design.

By 1985 I will have been an ordained Baptist minister thirty years. This material has been brought together and used over the span of those years. It is arbitrarily selected. Another book or two of the same design with totally different material could as well have been written. I have tried to be as accurate as possible in references to the sources. Since this is a resource book, the materials in it have been selected for their usefulness. Preachers are both invited and encouraged to use them.

The University Baptist Church, Fort Worth, Texas, where I serve as the book is prepared, constantly challenges me to do my very best preaching. For this I am grateful, as well as for their willingness to also let me write. The churches I have served as pastor, the preachers with whom I have had fellowship, the teachers who have guided my thoughts, and the pastors who have served as models all contributed to the book. The book, in fact, is dedicated to my pastor during my formative teenage years who was killed in Alaska by a careening automobile as he crossed a street to make a witnessing visit in an interim pastorate following his retirement. My family, especially my wife Carole, always encourages me in writing. This manuscript was prepared by Mrs. Pat Bohanan, pastor's secretary, University Baptist Church, Fort Worth, Texas, to whom I am deeply indebted and very grateful.

It is my prayer that this book prepared in the pressure of an active pastorate by a practicing preacher may be used by other preachers in a way that will honor God and advance His kingdom through the preaching of evangelistic messages.

JAMES E. CARTER

Pastor's Study
University Baptist Church
Fort Worth, Texas

PART I
Some Evangelistic Sermons

1
What Christ Did on the Cross

Colossians 2:13-15

For many people there is one distinctive, decisive act that makes them known to others. John Bunyan was a little-known preacher with Baptist convictions in seventeenth-century England. He was locked up in Bedford jail for preaching his "heretical" doctrines. Jailed but not silent, he wrote that immortal allegory, *The Pilgrim's Progress.* He has been known for over three hundred years for that one distinctive act.

Paul Revere was a silversmith in Colonial America. Yet he is hardly known for his ability as a silversmith. As when Henry Wadsworth Longfellow said:

> Listen, my children, and you shall hear
> Of the midnight ride of Paul Revere,
> On the eighteenth of April, in Seventy-five;
> Hardly a man is now alive
> Who remembers that famous day and year.

He was not talking about Revere's silversmithing. Paul Revere has been known to America by one distinctive act of patriotism.

In World War I, Alvin York was a mountain boy who made sergeant. Then overnight he was known around the world for his single-handed capture of a great number of the enemy. A book was written; a movie was made about his life. Sergeant York became a familiar name and legend. It was because of one distinctive act of heroism.

There is an act on the part of another that is more

distinctive than these. Its effects are more far-reaching than any of these. The one who acted has become so well known that He has changed human history and divided human time. No danger exists of His ever being forgotten. This is the act of Jesus on the cross, the act whereby the Son of God died for the sins of all people. Of the many acts of Jesus, each of which was filled with meaning and significance, the one that stands out in the minds of most of us is His act on the cross—His death for us.

What Jesus did on the cross has continued to be a mighty force in the lives of many persons. We hardly know how to describe it. The Bible tells about it in many vivid and colorful statements. W. Boyd Hunt described Paul's attempts at describing the cross in the *Encyclopedia of Southern Baptists*, (Vol. I, p. 92). He observed that Paul's glorying in the cross beggared language. He borrowed images from varied and widely-separated areas of life: "from the slave market, redemption; from the law court, justification; from war, reconciliation; from death, making alive; from the family and the law court, adoption; from commercial debt, forgiveness; from horticulture, engrafting; from ritual, washing." Language is strained to the breaking point in an attempt to describe this act of God.

One of the most vivid descriptions of Christ's great deed is found in the second chapter of Colossians. The Book of Colossians was written to combat a heresy that was playing down both the person and the work of Christ. They did not say that Jesus was not a person, but they deemphasized Him by saying that He was just one of many creatures graduated down from God until you get to man. They did not say that Jesus had not died on the cross. But they did say that alone was not sufficient for salvation.

To combat these two false ideas there are two doctrinal sections of the book. One deals with the supremacy of Christ and the other deals with the sufficiency of Christ.

This passage fits into the section dealing with the sufficiency of Christ. It tells us in remarkably vivid fashion what Christ did on the cross.

On the Cross Christ Forgave Our Committed Sins

What did Christ do on the cross? On the cross, Christ forgave our committed sins. Of our sin there can be no doubt.

The Scripture describes us as spiritually dead because of our sins. "Being dead in your sins" is the expression that is used. This word for *sin* describes the individual acts of sin. There is another word which emphasized the sin principle. This word means "to fall aside, to slip, to trespass." Perhaps "transgressions" would help us understand it better.

Because of these acts of sin we are dead. This is a basic principle of sin—it kills. Sin kills decency, self-respect, regard for others, sensitivity, desires for right living. Sin kills the very things we should desire most.

It has been said that Charles Darwin had a love for music. He had always planned to cultivate that interest in music and enjoy it after he retired. But he found that after years of giving all of his attention to scientific matters and no attention to music that his appreciation for it had been killed. When we direct our attention solely to the matters of self-gratification, it kills our desires and abilities to respond to spiritual things.

But we were also alienated from God because of our nature. "And the uncircumcision of your flesh" expresses the fleshly nature. We are by nature alienated from God. The principle of sin and rebellion becomes a part of the human nature. There is a definite gap between the created and the Creator. This gap has been immeasurably widened by our choice of sin. Our sinful nature and God's holy nature are not compatible. This has alienated us further from God. Something had to be done to reconcile us to God, to bring us back to the God who had given us life and promised us new life.

This was done by Christ on the cross. We can be wondrously made alive by His forgiveness that has been brought by the cross. "Quickened" means "made alive." "And you . . . hath he quickened together with him" the Scripture states. How? "Having forgiven you all trespasses" (Col. 2:13).

What a tremendous picture this is! We were spiritually dead because of our acts of sin; alienated from God by our sinful nature; but, as Christ was made alive in the resurrection, so has He made each of us alive by the forgiveness of those same sins.

Forgiveness does not erase the fact of sin. It does not even remove its consequences. But forgiveness does restore our relationship with God which had been marred by the sinful nature within us, from which had come conscious acts of sin. By the cross, Jesus provided forgiveness for us. The relationship with God can be restored.

On the Cross Christ Cancelled Our Assumed Debt

What did Christ do on the cross? On the cross He canceled our assumed debt. Colossians 2:14 reads, "Blotting out the handwriting of ordinances that was against us." "Ordinances" is translated by the ASV "bond," but Charles B. Williams translates it in a term that our credit-crazy generation can understand, "note." This refers specifically to the Mosaic law, but could be understood to refer generally to any legalistic requirement for right standing with God. One heretical strain, recognized in the New Testament, claimed that salvation was not just by the forgiveness of Christ by His act on the cross but also required keeping parts of the Mosaic law. They made a legal requirement of salvation. Paul replied that this was not so. Salvation is by grace. And in descriptive language he showed how Jesus had forever cleared away legal requirements for salvation which he characterized as a "note."

The debt was against us. Our sin and our own attempts at clearing away the debt of our sin by whatever legal manner taken is clearly against us. It is a bill of indebtedness which bears unmistakably our own signature. It is a valid claim. This note that was against us, "contrary to us," was as a bill of indebtedness which we cannot deny. It is as though a note had come due and we could not make the payment. The note became an enemy.

What, then, did Christ do to that note? He blotted it out. The word is sometimes used for "marking through." He marked through the debt that was against us. It is as though "Paid in Full" had been written across the account of our sin. But not only did He blot it out, He also took it away and nailed it to the cross. Among the things nailed to the cross when Jesus was crucified was the debt of our sin. By His death on that cross, Jesus completely paid the price of our sin. Our debt, which was valid and contrary to us, was taken away by Christ and nailed to the cross.

When I was nine years old I joined the YMCA in the summer. One of my friends who lived about a block or two away would go with me three days a week to the "Y" to play and to swim. A little bus that connected with the trolley line that took us to town ran right in front of my house. So each time we would go to the "Y" we were given enough money to ride the bus to the trolley and then to town and back home again.

One day my friend's mother gave him an extra dime and told him that we could get something refreshing to drink after we were dismissed. It seemed that session would never end. As soon as we had completed the swimming period and dressed, we hurried to the corner drugstore.

We crawled up on the stools at the lunch counter in that cool, air-conditioned store and prepared to make our order. Then we looked above the counter and saw those pictures that some master artist had painted depicting the various choices for food and refreshment available. One thing particularly took our eyes—a chocolate ice cream soda. We had no idea what they cost. If there ever was a case of "oversell" that was it. We were convinced that our day would not be complete without a chocolate ice cream soda. So we each ordered one; neither having had one before.

They lived up to our expectations. I do not think I have ever had anything quite so good. Then the waitress brought our ticket.

When we looked at the ticket we nearly died! The place suddenly got hot. Our appetite suddenly vanished. The soda turned sour. The ticket was for fifty cents and all we had was ten cents! I could just see myself washing dishes all night long at the drugstore to pay that ticket. We did not have any idea what to do. Then, just when we had sunk to our lowest, a man's hand reached between us, picked up the ticket, and a voice said, "That's all right, boys, I'll take care of this." Some unknown benefactor, whom we had never seen before nor since, paid our debt and rescued us.

In picturesque terms that is what Christ did for us on the cross. We had a valid debt with our sin. It was contrary to us. All of our legal manipulations could not cancel it. But Christ took it Himself. He blotted it out. He nailed it to the cross. And we have been rescued! We have been forgiven! Our relationship with God has been restored! We have new life! On the cross Christ canceled our assumed debt.

On the Cross Christ Destroyed Our Adverse Power

What did Christ do on the cross? On the cross, Christ destroyed our adverse power. Colossians 2:15, says, "And having spoiled principalities and powers, he made a shew of them openly, triumphing over them in it." "Principalities and powers" refer to the power of evil in the world.

It is sometimes considered to be the power of evil as personified in the devil. From the context, we would imagine that Paul was referring specifically to the power of the law that had kept people in bondage rather than liberating them to serve God. We could properly, I think, apply this to any adverse power that would hinder us from realizing our potential for Christ, specifically the power of evil in our lives.

And how did Christ destroy the adverse power? He stripped the power of evil of all its power. "Spoiled" is the word that is used. By the cross and the resurrection, Jesus stripped evil and death of all its power. What had been intended as a defeat of Him became instead a defeat of the power of evil.

Not only did Jesus strip evil of its power, He also made a spectacle of it. When these words were read by first-century Christians they would probably immediately think of a Roman triumph. A conqueror would enter the city of Rome in a triumphal entry. The people would all turn out. The streets would be lined with expectant throngs. The people would cheer as the procession would come into view. First would come the legions, then the cavalry with the soldiers on beautiful horses, next the chariots with the charioteers looking arrogantly across the crowd. In the midst of the chariots, like a god, would be the conqueror himself, the general of the victorious army. Behind him would come the trophies of war. Slaves would bear the wealth of the conquered city or nation.

Last would come the captured people—once proud, now slaves—trudging by with their shoulders bent and their faces downcast. These were the true spoils of victory. A public spectacle was being made of these people. His triumph was a reminder that they had been defeated and disarmed. So Christ has made a public spectacle of the powers of sin, Satan, and evil by His triumph of the cross.

Christ has triumphed over all the powers of evil on the

cross. That which was supposed to be an instrument of shame was instead an instrument of glory and victory.

But why do we not know more of this victory, this defeat of sin, and the power of evil? We can have this same sense of victory to the extent that the cross is applied to our lives. To the extent that we let Christ live in our lives and triumph over us, we can know of the defeat of evil. The last battle has not been fought. The war is far from over. But the final outcome is known already. Because of the death of Christ on the cross and the resurrection of Christ from the dead, we know what the final outcome will be. In the end, evil has been decisively destroyed. In the end, sin has been conquered. In the end, Satan has been set down. Christ has done this through His death and resurrection. We do not have to be controlled by sin. We can be controlled by God's love. Christ has won a decisive victory and we can share in it by faith.

Early in 1972 Shoichi Yokoi was captured in the jungles of Guam. Rather than surrender to the American enemy he held out for twenty-eight years in the jungle, according to a news report. He was captured by Guamanians near his jungle hideout where he had lived in a tunnel eating breadfruit, coconuts, snails, rats' livers, shrimp, frogs, and fish. He kept track of time by marking a tree trunk every full moon.

He was aware of Japan's surrender in World War II from leaflets and newspapers scattered about the island. But *he* refused to surrender.

This man may be a modern parable. All around us are people who will not recognize the victory was on Calvary. The victory of Christ over the powers that are adverse to us can be known if we will come out of hiding to the light; if we will come from out dependence on self to faith in Christ.

What a distinctive act Christ performed on the cross! He forgave our sins, thus giving life. He canceled our debts, thus giving freedom. He triumphed over the power of evil, thus giving victory. And it was all done for you! This is the act that provides salvation as Christ is accepted as personal Savior.

2
What It Means to Be Lost

Ephesians 2:1-3

One of the mystifying remainders of the Vietnam War is the persons who are MIA (missing in action). Their families, and even their government in some cases, believe and hope that they are alive. But they are lost from them. They are separated from those who love them. In a general sense, it is known where they are, but they are still lost.

Occasionally, we will see on the evening news reports on television about a mine cave-in somewhere. People are trapped in a tunnel. They know approximately where they are but are unable to reach them even though they drill escape holes and try to communicate with them. We can feel some of the anguish of their loved ones as they gather hour by hour at the entrance to the mine. Even though their whereabouts are generally known, they are lost to their families and friends. They are separated from them.

In our rather specialized religious vocabulary we talk about people being lost. What does it mean to be lost? These are people we know. They may be family members, or work associates, or neighbors. We know them and we know where they are. But because they do not know Jesus Christ as Savior we call them lost. They are separated from God. They are lost to God and to His salvation. But what does it mean to be lost?

For an answer, there is no better place to turn than the second chapter of Ephesians. There we have a vivid de-

scription of what it means to be lost. This section follows
Paul's great hymn of praise that describes the plan of
redemption. In this Paul showed what God had done for
believers through Christ. For this consideration they first
showed what the believers were without Christ. This is
what it means to be lost.

Spiritually Dead

What does it mean to be lost? To be lost is to be spiritually dead. Paul described the condition in verse 1, as "dead
in trespasses and sin." there is no better way to describe
the condition of the lost person than one who is spiritually
dead. "Lost" means insensitive and completely cut off
from the spiritual life and power which we find in Christ.
Verse 1 stands in contrast with verse 10. The plan of God
for each of us is that we should walk in spiritual life and
good works. But the actual fact is that those who have not
trusted Christ as Savior—have not given their hearts and
lives to Him in faith commitment, have not asked Him for
forgiveness of sins and new birth—are spiritually dead.

So the condition of the lost person is death. It has been
occasioned through trespasses and sins. This is the realm
of death—the realm of sin and trespasses. *Sin* is the more
general word. *Trespasses* is the word for specific sins. Sin
means basically "missing the mark." We sin when we miss
the mark that God has set up for us. When our life is less
than it ought to be or should be, we have sinned. Trespass
means basically a "slip or fall." This has reference more to
the specific acts of sin and evil. This is taking the wrong
road when we could have taken the right road.

How vividly and completely this describes our condition in sin! The person who is dead, spiritually dead, because of his sins has in his life the general habit of sin out
of which issues the specific acts of sin. Because of the habit
of sin in the life, it is possible for one to commit the
specific acts of sin. So we needn't go around saying that
any one of us is without sin because we have omitted the

specific sinful acts that are so obvious to all. All have need of salvation because of the general condition of sinfulness, of missing the mark, that we have. This is what brings about spiritual death: the sins and trespasses which kill all spiritual sensitivity.

And this is exactly what the Bible tells us in other places. This is the end result of sin—the wages of sin. Very plainly Paul stated in Romans 6:23 "For the wages of sin is death." This is the pay that one gets for his sinful life and living. It is eternal death, separation from God and from all that's good and holy in the life to come. But in this life, at this time, it is spiritual death. It is a living death. Alive, and yet dead, because of sin and trespasses.

In his famous sermon, "Payday—Someday," R.G. Lee told of the man who called him one day identifying himself as "The Chief of the Kangaroo Court." Lee at that time was pastor of the First Baptist Church, New Orleans, Louisiana. "The Chief of the Kangaroo Court" told Lee that all of that stuff he was preaching was nonsense, that God didn't exist, and that what he described as sin was just good living. From time to time after that he would get phone calls, some in the morning, others in the afternoon, some late at night, some at the office at the church, others at his home. But each of the calls from the "Chief of the Kangaroo Court" would taunt him, ridicule him, and laugh at his ideas of sin, judgment, and God's accounting in life.

Then one day he got a call from the big New Orleans Charity Hospital. They said that they had a man there who was about to die. He was out of his mind and raving but had asked for Dr. Lee. He had said something about being "The Chief of the Kangaroo Court." Immediately Dr. Lee rushed over. He was led to him and saw for the first time the man he had talked with several times. The man was the very picture of one in whom sin had evidently taken its toll. As Dr. Lee tried to talk to him, he said, "The devil pays off all right—but he pays in counterfeit money, he pays in counterfeit money." And with these words he was gone to meet the God whom he had scoffed. He had lived long enough to give credit to what the Scripture plainly teaches us: the wages of sin is death.

Helplessly Enslaved

To be lost is to be helplessly enslaved. Several phrases in verses 2-3 show that condition.

Enslaved by the spirit of the age is one element of it. Paul expressed that with ". . . walked according to the course of this world."

"Spirit of the age" translates "course of this world" into terms that we can understand better. The existence of the one who is lost is not determined by his freedom of choice as he thinks it is. Rather it is determined by the spirit of the world in which he lives.

Think of the things that would characterize the spirit of our age: greed, lust, unrestrained and undisciplined action, selfishness, the will to power. And when you look around you it is easy to understand that this is exactly the spirit which has captured so many. Greed is the basis of widespread personal and public corruption. Lust helps to explain the very low moral standards. Lack of restraint and discipline is seen in every schoolroom in the country.

Selfishness is revealed on every hand. Rather than asking, "What can I do to help the world in which I live," the usual question is "What can I do to help myself." Because of selfishness personal relations break down, embezzlement is carried on, and cheating occurs. The will to power is seen as people fight and struggle to get recognition in school clubs, social organizations, service and civic clubs, even international politics.

This is something of the spirit of the age. And this spirit catches those who are subject to it and carries them to its own awful destination—lost before God.

Enslaved by the power of Satan is the condition of the

lost person. Paul showed that with the phrase "according to the prince of the power of the air."

The people of Paul's day believed that the air was filled with evil spirits. These spirits were ruled by the prince of the power of the air—the devil himself. We have relegated the devil in our day to the cartoons and the caricatures. If we were really honest we would admit that there seems to be a power of evil loose in the world. You will notice that the spirit of the age is directed by the prince of the power of the air. Satan has worked his way into the hearts of so many that they believe they are making their own choices when actually even the choices of life are directed by the devil himself.

The German preacher, Helmut Thielicke, related a very interesting experiment in his book, *How the World Began.* Some of his students at the University of Hamburg helped in volunteer service in a camp for refugees from East Germany. Each afternoon they would put on a Punch and Judy Show. Thielicke played the part of the devil.

He wielded a horrible, fiery red puppet in one hand and mustered up a menacing and horrible voice to represent all the terrible discords of hell. Then in tones brimming with sulphur he advised the children to indulge in every conceivable naughtiness: never to wash their feet at night; stick your tongue out at anybody you want to; be sure to drop banana skins on the street so people will slip on them. This sounds like a terrible thing to advise children. But the results were enormous and generally recognized in the camp. The children suddenly stopped sticking out their tongues and they also washed their feet at night. They actually shouted him down with ear-splitting protests when he handed out wicked suggestions. They would have absolutely no truck with the devil.

But there is one significant point at which Thielicke's Punch and Judy devil and temptation is different from our daily temptation: right from the start he let it be known by his mask and his voice that he was the devil. Because of this, his suggestions could never succeed. In our experience Satan works insidiously and slyly. He never identifies himself for what he is, and we have laughed at the cartoons so much that we have laughed him out of practical existence—right into practical control of our lives.

To be helplessly enslaved is to be enslaved by a spirit of rebellion. Paul called such persons "children of disobedience."

This is a typical Jewish way of saying that lives are characterized by disobedience. That is the very essence of sin, whether missing the mark or slipping or falling through trespasses, disobedience. From the time Adam and Eve disobeyed God in the Garden of Eden until now, disobedience is the heart of sin.

That the helplessly enslaved are enslaved by our own desires is indicated in verse 3. The desires of the flesh and the mind control the sinful life. Remember that "flesh" in the Bible and fleshly sins does not refer just to sexual sins. In Paul's list of sins of the flesh in Galatians 5:19-21 he includes with adultery and fornication, idolatry, hatred, wrath, strife, envyings, seditions, heresies.

The flesh is the lower part of our nature; the flesh is that part of our nature which gives sin a bridgehead and a point of attack. The meaning of the flesh will vary from person to person. One person's weakness may be in the body and his risk may be sexual sin. Another individual's sin may be in spiritual things and his risk may be in pride. Another one's sin may be in earthly things and his risk may be unworthy ambition. Another person's sin may be in his temper and his risk may be in envyings and strife. All are sins of the flesh.

Let no one think that, because he has escaped the grosser sins of the body, he has avoided the sins of the flesh. And let no one think, because her body is hard to control, that she is the only one who is fighting with the sins of the flesh. The flesh is anything in us which gives sin its chance;

it is human nature without God. To live according to the dictates of the flesh is simply to live in such a way that our lower nature, the worse part of us, dominates our lives.

An Object of Wrath

To be lost is to be an object of God's wrath. "And were by nature children of wrath," is the way the Scripture expresses it. How vividly this expresses the fact that those who are lost and without Christ await the wrath of God and are objects of His wrath. The wrath of God is not a capricious thing. In the New Testament the "wrath of God" refers to God's settled opposition to sin. It pictures the fixed displeasure of God to sin.

Whenever one has chosen the way of sin and of rebellion as his way of life, then he is inviting the wrath of God to fall upon him. This is his own choice. He could choose to follow Christ in salvation and walk according to God's will and to good works, but instead he chooses to follow the direction of the spirit of the age and its ruler, Satan. Because of this, the fixed displeasure of God becomes his part in life. John expressed it very well when he said, "He that believeth on the Son hath everlasting life: and he that believeth not the Son shall not see life; but the wrath of God" (3:36), because of their rebellion and their sin and because of God's nature of holiness are known as children of wrath.

Part of the wrath of God is revealed in this life. Look to the person whose life has been lived in sin. He has become coarse, hardened, and insensitive. The wrath of God as a natural result of his sin has caused him to lose much of that which is finest and best in life. He has become insensitive even to the voice of God and the wooing of the Holy Spirit of God.

But there is also a future aspect of the wrath of God. All of God's wrath is not realized here on earth. Sin has its natural consequences all right. But wrath is also meted out at a future date. The Bible assures a judgment of God upon our sin. And the Bible also assures us that those who are lost and have not trusted Christ as Savior are consigned to hell for eternity. God's wrath, His opposition to sin, is finally settled in hell. This is the extreme limit to which God will go in opposing sin. The person who is lost is by nature a child of wrath, an object of God's wrath.

This is what it means to be lost. It means being spiritually dead, helplessly enslaved, an object of wrath.

But, thank God, that is not all of it. One doesn't have to remain lost. One can be saved. A person can be saved by the grace of God and the death of Jesus Christ His Son. Verses 1 through 3 describe the condition of the lost. But verse 4 begins "But God . . ." and describes something of the mercy and grace of God that saves us from this condition of being lost and promises us eternal life with Him.

B. H. Carroll was a giant of a man, both physically and spiritually. One of twelve children, his father was a Baptist preacher who had come to Texas by way of Mississippi and Arkansas. As a student at Baylor University he had debated against Texas entering the Confederacy in the Civil War. Yet at eighteen he enlisted and fought in the war. At the Battle of Mansfield (Louisiana) where the Confederates beat back the Union forces, Carroll was wounded in the leg.

At twenty-two years of age, still on crutches from his war wound, B. H. Carroll, scoffing at the Christianity his father had preached, went to a revival service held under a wooden shed in Caldwell, Texas. The sermon was a failure. But the preacher looked right into the eyes of the big man draped over his crutches standing on the outskirts of the crowd and challenged, "You that stand aloof from Christianity and scorn us simple folks, what have you got?"

The simple logic of the question stung Carroll. His heart answered the question by saying that he had nothing under the whole heaven, absolutely nothing. As he hobbled forward to the altar he was not prepared for the effect it would have on the congregation. Some began even to shout. He warned them that he wasn't converted, he was just going to give religion a test. But some of the women remained to sing and to praise God over his turnaround. That touched him. Suddenly there flashed into the mind of that man, who later regularly read one thousand pages a day for nearly half a century and could quote verbatim chapters of books he had read thirty years before, a verse of Scripture: "Come unto me, all ye that labour and are heavy laden, and I will give you rest" (Matt. 12:29).

It was as though he saw Christ himself standing before him. He cast himself for all time at the feet of Jesus. At that moment he received an indescribable and unspeakable rest that remained with him the rest of his life.

The rest of Carroll's life was devoted to the service of Christ. For twenty-nine years he was pastor of the First Baptist Church, Waco, Texas. He was president of the board of trustees of Baylor University for more than twenty years. He wrote a thirteen-volume *Interpretation of the English Bible,* among other works. And he was the founder of Southwestern Baptist Theological Seminary. In Jesus Christ he found cleansing from his scoffing, rejecting sin and was given new life.

And anyone who comes to Jesus can be saved. You do not have to be lost. You can be saved. You can be changed from spiritual death, from hopeless enslavement, and from the prospect of God's wrath to a new person in Christ Jesus. Faith in Christ makes the difference. Come to faith in Christ and pass from death to life.

3
What It Means to Be Saved

1 Corinthians 6:9-11

In Houston, Texas, in one of Billy Graham's evangelistic crusades, a man was saved. He owned a liquor store. The next morning he had a sign on the front of the door saying, "Out of business." He had been saved and he couldn't carry on the same kind of business as before.

I read of a man some time ago who had been saved in an evangelistic service. He was known as the city drunk. He was called "Old John." Somebody spoke to him the next morning on the street and said, "Good morning, Old John." He said, "Who are you talking to? My name is not Old John. I'm *new* John." He had been saved and a complete revolution had taken place in his life.

I heard about a man in a Texas town who used to hitch his horse every morning in front of the saloon. One morning the saloon-keeper came out and found that the horse was hitched in front of the Methodist Church. He saw the man walking down the street and called out, "Say, why is your horse hitched in front of the Methodist Church this morning?" The man turned around and said, "Well, last night I was converted in the revival meeting, and I've changed hitching posts." He had been saved, born again, converted, and he had changed hitching posts. No longer was his life hitched to sin, but now to the Savior.

These three things related in Billy Graham's book, *Peace with God,* tell us something about what it means to be saved. To be saved means to change your way of life, it means a change in the very nature of life, and it means hitching yourself in faith to God for deliverance and well-being.

In three verses of the sixth chapter of 1 Corinthians Paul expressed pretty well what it means to be saved. The immediate context of verses 9-11 is the problem of Christian people going to court in lawsuits against one another. Paul told them that this ought not to be. Why, they, with Christ, would some day judge the world. And it is utterly wrong to take matters to be judged to the unrighteous to judge between Christians when one sees what the unrighteous really are. In verses 9 and 10 the apostle told of the sins of the unrighteous. They are sins against self: sexual sins of all kinds and idolatry and sins against others. "And such were some of you" Paul said. "But ye are ..." is the rest of the sentence. And that is important. This points up very well what it means to be saved.

Cleansed from Sin

To be saved means to be cleansed from sin. Paul said, "but ye are washed"

This word "but" is the strongest kind of adversative. It is used to show a clean break between what has gone before and what follows. "And such were some of you" describes the sorry condition of sin in which the sinner finds himself before God's grace activates his heart. "But ye are" stands in firm contrast with what has gone before.

How vividly this expresses the nature of salvation. It is a clean break with the past of sin. It is a great contrast between the life of sin and the life of grace in Christ.

The root meaning of the word *salvation* is deliverance or preservation from danger. And this is exactly what God has done for us in the salvation which we enjoy in Christ: He has delivered us from sin and preserved us from the danger that sin brings in ultimate destruction and ruin. And one very vivid way of expressing this salvation is that it is a cleansing from our sin.

Cleansing from sin is the forgiveness of sins. When

Christ saves us He forgives us of our sins. Ephesians 1:7 equates forgiveness and redemption. It says, "In whom we have redemption through his blood, the forgiveness of sins, according to the riches of his grace." So this is what it means to be cleansed of sin—it means to be forgiven of sin.

The first step in forgiveness of sin is to realize our need of forgiveness. Reinhold Niebuhr has said that no cumulation of contradictory evidence seems to disturb modern man's good opinion of himself. And this is our greatest problem in salvation: to realize that we really need salvation. To experience forgiveness, you must look into the depths of your own heart of sin and realize that you have sinned against God and that sin must be forgiven.

But quickly someone says, "I read that list of sins Paul wrote in 1 Corinthians 6:9-10, I'm not any of those. I have never committed any of those vile things." Don't think for a moment that excuses you before God. The only sin that condemns a guilty sinner is the sin of unbelief. Didn't you notice that of all those other awful categories of sin he said, "And such *were* some of you" (italics mine). *Were* is an important word. They were those things, but now they have had their sin forgiven. God can forgive us of any sin, but as long as we refuse to believe on Him as Savior and ask for forgiveness there is no forgiveness of sin no matter how sterling the character or how clean the life. John expressed it clearly when he said, "He that believeth on him is not condemned: but he that believeth not is condemned already, because he hath not believed in the name of the only begotten Son of God" (John 3:18). So into our consciousness there must come the realization that we have sinned and stand even now in need of forgiveness, cleansing from that sin.

But how does this forgiveness come about? Revelation 1:5 refers to Jesus as the one who loved us and washed us from our sins in His own blood. This is exactly how forgiveness and cleansing of sin comes about. Jesus loved us enough to die on the cross for us. And by His death on the cross we can have forgiveness of these sins if we trust in Him to forgive us and to cleanse us.

A preacher once asked a dying woman if she had made her peace with God. She said no. "Do you realize," he said, "that you are dying and that soon you must go out to face God and give an account of your life?" "Yes," replied the woman, "but I am not disturbed about that. I do not have to make my peace with God; Christ made that peace for me on Calvary nineteen hundred years ago. I am simply resting in the peace which he has already made." Christ has already made peace for us. We have to enter into that peace through faith and receive the peace of God which is the forgiveness of sin and the cleansing from sin.

Set Apart for Service

To be saved means to be set apart for service. Paul assured the Ephesians by saying "But ye are sanctified."

When you are saved you are forgiven of your sins. But also along with forgiveness there is *sanctification.* Now this is a word of which we have been afraid. It has been misused and abused by so many people that we have often shied away from it. It is a good Bible word. And it has a good Bible meaning. The basic meaning of sanctification is to separate or set apart. When something is sanctified it is set aside, separated, set apart.

And this is exactly what God does for us when He saves us: He sets us apart for His use and His service. The verb tense for this word is the same as for "washed." This means that this, too, is a decisive action which God has taken at one point. At the time of our faith and belief in Christ God not only forgives us of our sin but He also sets us apart for Himself.

When America entered World War II, her great automobile plants were changed from peacetime production to wartime production. Instead of making automobiles, they began to make planes and tanks. In other words, they were set apart for a new type of work; the entire purpose of their machines was changed. And so it is that when you are saved, the purpose of your life is changed, and no longer are you to serve sin. You have been set aside to serve God.

Sanctification, then, is a definite act on the part of God at the time a person is saved. You are set apart at that time for service to God.

But sanctification is also used as the process of growth which the Christian experiences. Sanctification is not only an act but also a process. We are to grow in grace. As we come to know more about God, more about His word, and more about His standards and demands, then we ought to grow more and more to meet Him and His standards.

But the tragic part of it is that so many have forgotten all about being sanctified. They are saved and like to remember that means that you don't go to hell. But at the same time you are saved you are sanctified—and that means that you have been set apart for God's service. Set apart for God's service and use. If you look on salvation as nothing more than fire insurance from hell, then you have an absolutely warped idea of salvation. Sanctification is one part of it—and that means that in an act and in a process you are to serve God. We grow in grace and sanctification—to be more like Jesus—by prayer, by Bible study, by faithfulness to duty, by conscious effort to pattern our lives after the life of the Master.

Made Just by God

To be saved means to be made just by God. Paul also said, "But ye are justified."

Justification is another term used by Paul to express our salvation. Just as God forgives and sets apart so does He justify those who have accepted Christ as personal Savior. This is a legal term used in a vital sense. It means basically to show right or to pronounce right. But this does not catch all that is involved in it. God doesn't just pronounce us right, He makes us right. This is the very nature of salvation and the new birth. In this, God does for us what we cannot do for ourselves. We could never make ourselves just or right. But God can. And that is what He does in our hearts and lives at the time we accept Christ as Savior. We are made right before God.

Be sure to notice that it is sinners who are made just by God. Recall the list of perverted personalities named in verses 9 and 10. These are the very people that he is now saying have been made just and right through faith in Jesus Christ. Turn back in your Bibles to the third chapter of Romans. We see that Paul had taken great pains to show that both Jews and Greeks had sinned and did not have righteousness before God. He made that pronouncement that includes us all in sin: "For there is no difference: For all have sinned and come short of the glory of God" (vv.:22*b*-23). But then he followed that with the glorious words, "Being justified freely by his grace through the redemption that is in Christ Jesus" (v. 24).

In no better fashion could this great truth have been presented. We have all sinned. There is no one of us who could say that he has not risen up in rebellion and disobedience before God. But God justifies us when we are sinners. We are justified freely by His grace. What grace that is! What wonder that is! We have sinned against God, and it is God Himself who makes us just and right through redemption by His grace.

And this also points us to another aspect of justification: it is by faith. Paul contrasted justification by works and justification by faith. We are justified, made right and just before God, on the condition of our faith in Him—not in anything that we do. This is one thing that often throws off good moral persons who are not Christians. They say, "Well, since I have been a good moral person, and I have not fallen into any of those grievous errors condemned by

Paul in verses 9 and 10, and I treat my family well, that will entitle me to salvation."

But that is missing the whole mark. Being a good moral person does entitle you to something. It entitles you to respect and honor and a good reputation. But it doesn't entitle you to salvation. This is an attempt to work one's way to justification pure and simple. But this is not justification. Justification is by faith not by our works. When Martin Luther was climbing the Scala Sancta, the sacred stairs in Rome, kissing every step as it was prescribed, he remembered the words of the Scripture "The just shall live by faith." He then stood up and walked down the stairs. This became the battle cry of the Reformation, "The just shall live by faith." And this catches up the emphasis of the Scripture. We cannot earn or work for our salvation. Justification comes by faith in Jesus Christ as personal savior.

So then, this being true, justification by faith is based on Christ's work for us. Notice how we are washed and sanctified and justified. It is done "in the name of the Lord Jesus, and by the Spirit of our God" (v. 11). In the name of Jesus: it is based on the work that Jesus has done in dying for our sins on the cross. In the spirit of God: the Holy Spirit makes effective this justification in our hearts and lives when we accept Christ by faith. As Paul told us in Romans, justification is the gift of God given freely to us. This does not mean that it didn't cost anything. It cost Christ His life. But God gives it to us freely upon our acceptance of it in faith.

A preacher tried to explain to a miner that salvation is a free gift of God. The miner could not understand it in this way. One day the preacher accompanied him to the mines. They were preparing to descend several hundred feet by the company elevator, when the preacher said to the miner, "How much will this cost me?"

The miner replied, "It will cost you nothing."

"That is too cheap," the preacher said. "I don't want to ride on anything that costs nothing."

"Cheap!" exclaimed the miner. "This elevator cost $25,000—the company paid that much for it."

"Oh," said the preacher, "I understand—it costs me nothing but it did cost someone else a great price." So he was able to explain to the miner that salvation came to us in the same manner. It cost someone else a great price. It cost us nothing, but it did cost another a great price—it cost Christ all that He had. And this is justification. It is based on Christ's work and our appropriation of that work to ourselves.

Justification, then, is God's act of making sinners righteous when, by faith, they accept the work of Christ.

This is what it means to be saved. Forgiveness and sanctification and justification are all different aspects of the same act. This experience can be yours. Accept Christ by faith.

4
Where the Need Is

Jeremiah 17:9-10

There is a man who is now living in retirement in Florida who was very good at what he did in his more active days. He broke into banks and broke out of prisons. Willie "The Actor" Sutton is credited with having robbed 100 banks and having escaped from three prisons, two of them considered inescapable. Even though in his autobiography, *Where the Money Is,* Willie Sutton denied ever having said it, but admitted that it is what he would have said, there is a familiar quotation credited to him. Supposedly Willie Sutton was once asked why he robbed banks. He said, "Because that's where the money is."

Suppose we were to pose the question to ourselves, "Why do I come to church and expose my heart to God?" In our better moments we might reply, "Because that is where my need is."

Push it back further and ask the question of God, "Why did you send your Son Jesus Christ to earth to die on the cross for sinful human beings?" And His answer could well be; "Because that is where the need is."

Jeremiah the prophet framed the question for us. It was in those perilous days prior to the fall of Jerusalem that Jeremiah the spokesman for God centered the rebelliousness and self-will and deception and emptiness upon the people themselves. Their hearts were not right. It is well-said in Jeremiah 17:9: "The heart is deceitful above all things and desperately wicked: who can know it?"

For the Hebrew the heart was not the seat of emotion

43

but of intellect and will. It was the center of life where the decisions of will were made. It was the place of decision making. We may speak of the heart in emotional terms. For the Hebrews the heart was considered more in volitional terms. That was where the decision was made.

This being true, anything of a permanent nature that is done to a human being will have to be done to the heart. That is where the need is. Dag Hammarskjold once noted that the only hope for peace is in the human heart.

Why did Christ die on the cross? To change the heart and give new life to persons because that is where the need is!

Why did God love us enough to send his Son Jesus Christ to earth to become one of us and to die for us? To give human beings heart and to show the extent of His love to us because that is where the need is!

Why do we worship God today? We come before God in worship and openness and lay ourselves bare before God. We do that so God can change our hearts, because that is where the need is!

Where is the need of humanity centered today? It is centered in the very same place that it was in the days of the prophet Jeremiah: in the human heart.

Disclaimer

When we say that the human heart is where the need of salvation, change, and new life is we have to begin the discussion with a disclaimer. The disclaimer is that Christian theology does not say that all people are as bad as they can be. Total depravity does not mean that everyone is so totally depraved that there is nothing of worth or value in them. It does not mean that everything about everybody is bad and terrible.

Rather, the doctrine of total depravity does affirm at least three things. The first thing that it affirms is that all persons are sinners both by nature and by choice. Romans 3:23 reminds us, "For all have sinned, and come short of the glory of God." A second thing that the doctrine of human depravity affirms is that all things touched by human hands are dirtied and made wrong. We have the capability of even turning good things into bad things. The third affirmation, and the cornerstone of that doctrine, is that persons cannot save themselves. We are totally incapable of delivering ourselves from sin. Deliverance from sin must come from the hands of God.

That human hands have dirtied the things they touch can be demonstrated in various ways. Notice some of those expressions of our sinfulness.

We can see it in the way we govern ourselves. Americans believe very strongly that democracy is the best form of government. But we built a system of checks and balances into the United States Constitution. That was done in recognition of the fact that while power corrupts, absolute power corrupts absolutely. And our founding fathers were not interested in any person or any branch of government exercising undue power over others. Knowing the human proclivity to snatch and grab what is in reach and to turn even good things into instruments of evil, the Constitution itself has checks and balances to help us keep ourselves in check.

We can see it in the struggle for power and leadership. You really don't have to go any further than a Sunday School class or a local church to see people trying to grasp for power. Much of the problem that arises in a church, or any other human organization for that matter, is the struggle for power. On a larger level you can see it as people jockey for positions of leadership and prominence, not for the service they can render but for the power they can receive.

And look at the idealism that so many people had at one time. People begin their careers, their lives, their marriages with great and lofty ideals. But they soon turn into cynicism and maneuvering. There are people who began their ministries with great ideals of serving Christ and became only employees of churches. Teachers often start with wonderful ideals of advancing the frontiers of knowledge and serving humankind and end up keeping school. Marriages begin with high ideals of love and devotion and end up with both the mortgage and crabgrass. Our idealism is muddied by our sinfulness.

Consider tolerance also. What begins as tolerance toward others and their attitudes may soon turn into indifference that sees nothing as really right or wrong but all things as relative. A river can run so broad that it has no depth. And the tolerance that is admirable can become the indifference that is despicable.

Ernest Campbell, formerly pastor of Riverside Church in New York City and now a professor of homiletics, told the story of play between him and one of his golfing friends. Evidently both of them qualified as duffers rather than expert golfers. Many golfers take a mulligan, a second shot off the tee on the first hole of a round, Campbell confessed that he and his partner took mulligans on the first nine holes.

Then once on the green they were very liberal with the gimme, that shot where the ball is lying so close to the hole that it is assumed the player can stroke it in the hole. When a shot is a gimme it does not have to be hit.

With Campbell's ball lying about sixteen feet from the cup and his friend's ball about fourteen feet from the cup, Campbell would back off, take a hard look, and say to his buddy that he thought it was a gimme. Of course, the friend would not hit the ball but would just pick it up. It is terribly embarassing to go ahead and hit a gimme and then miss it. Then, out of kindness, the golfing partner would also look over to Campbell and profess that he believed his ball was a gimme, too. Can't you just imagine these two friends making their way easily around the golf course hitting mulligans and picking up gimmes? But then Campbell brought the point of the story home in a way that erased the smiles brought on by the thought of their loose play. He asked: "But who speaks for par?"

Indeed, if nothing really matters and life can go merrily along its way with nothing actually counting, what difference would it make? But golf is a game of skill because there is par, that which is expected of the golfer and that which challenges the player to his best. And life has expectations for us, too. And we have responsibilities, too. God does hold us accountable.

While we may not be the worst possible sinners, we do have to admit that there is something wrong at the center of the human heart. What is wrong is our sin in our hearts.

Description

If the heart is indeed the center of our need, how can we describe the human heart? Jeremiah gave three descriptions.

The human heart is deceitful.

Sin entered the human heart with deception. Genesis 3 tells the story of the entrance of sin into the human experience through deception.

That is also the way that sin remains here. We deceive ourselves if we think that it doesn't make any difference. We deceive ourselves when we think that we do not have to give an account for our lives and our choices. We deceive ourselves when we think that what we do will have no effect on others who count on us and trust us.

The Hebrew word for *deceit* is an interesting word. Literally, it means following the heel, dogging one's footsteps for the purpose of destroying that person. That is the word from which the name *Jacob* is derived. Jacob, you remember, was the deceiver. He spent his whole early life deceiving people: his brother, his father, his father-in-law. He was not the kind of person to admire. Deceit does that to an individual.

The human heart is also desperately wicked.

The human heart is so desperately wicked that we are

always devising ways to sin. We are trying to find new ways to assert ourselves. We look for the ways that we can gain advantage over other people or take advantage of situations.

Why do we do these things? It is because our hearts are corrupt. It is because we are basically sinners.

In Robert Penn Warren's novel *All the King's Men*, Willie Starks asked his associate Jack Burden to attempt to get Judge Irwin, a political opponent of Starks and an old family friend of Burden's, on Starks's side. In the conversation Starks told Burden that he was not asking him to frame Irwin. Then he asked Burden if he had ever asked him to frame anyone. When Burden replied that he had not, Starks then asked if he knew why he had never asked him to frame anyone. When Burden answered that he did not know, Starks responded by saying that it was never necessary. He said that you never had to frame anybody because the truth was sufficient.

The human heart is definitely beyond understanding. That is Jeremiah's third description of the heart: it is beyond understanding. We cannot even understand ourselves. We do not understand why our rebellion against God and our drive toward our self-will is so deep. Jeremiah gave one reason: it is deep-rooted. Note his description in the opening words of chapter 17. "The sin of Judah is written with a pen of iron, and with the point of a diamond: it is graven upon the table of their heart, and upon the horns of your altars" (v. 1).

I heard once of a salesman who dated a preacher's daughter. He decided he wanted a full report on her so he hired a private detective to give him a report. The report came back that she was of good reputation, gentle, refined, with many churchgoing friends. The only question mark was a salesman of doubtful reputation who had been seen with her lately.

When we really get down to looking at it we find some things about ourselves we can't understand. The complexity of the human heart and our self-willfulness is beyond understanding.

Deliverance

This being true—that the human heart is deceitful, corrupt, and beyond understanding—is there anything that can be done for us? Is there any deliverance from this condition?

Yes, there is. We can be delivered by having a new heart. Our hearts can be changed and totally made new through faith in Jesus Christ.

The very prophet who described the condition of the human heart also declared its deliverance. God can give a new heart. Heed the words of Jeremiah 31:31-34:

> Behold, the days come, said the Lord, that I will make a new covenant with the house of Israel and with the house of Judah:
> Not according to the covenant that I made with their fathers in the day that I took them by the hand to bring them out of the land of Egypt; which my covenant they brake, although I was an husband unto them, saith the Lord:
> But this shall be the covenant that I will make with the house of Israel; After those days, saith the Lord, I will put my law in their inward parts, and write it in their hearts; and will be their God, and they shall be my people.
> And they shall teach no more every man his neighbour, and every man his brother, saying, Know the Lord: for they shall all know me, from the least of them unto the greatest of them, saith the Lord: for I will forgive their iniquity, and I will remember their sin no more.

The prophet Ezekiel also picked up on the concept of the new heart and wrote: "And I will give them one heart, and I will put a new spirit within you: and I will take the stony heart out of their flesh, and will give them an heart of flesh: That they may walk in my statutes, and keep mine ordinances, and do them: and they shall be my people and I will be their God" (Ezek. 11:19-20).

The writer of the Book of Hebrews in the New Testament took the reference to the New Covenant and the new heart from Jeremiah and fitted it verbatim into his teaching of the New Covenant with Christ (Heb. 8:8-12).

Deliverance from the sinful, corrupt heart can come with a new heart attained through faith in Jesus Christ. The promise of God in being our God and our being his people has been fulfilled in Jesus Christ. We enter into that promise through faith in Christ.

Christian Baarnard, the South African surgeon who performed the world's first successful heart transplant, once said that it was a sin to bury a usable heart. God wants to give each one of us a usable heart, a heart that can be used in His service and dedicated to His glory.

How does that come about? It comes about by giving the heart in faith and commitment to Jesus Christ, the son of God who gave His life for us. Through faith in Christ God gives us a new heart and delivers us from our sin.

John Wesley was the founder of the Methodist Church. It got its name from their methodical way of studying and system of organization. While a student at Oxford University he joined a group formed by his brother, Charles, which concentrated on attendance at worship, regular hours of private prayer, visitation of the sick, and a strict moral code. The other students ridiculed it by calling it the "Holy Club" and other affectionate names.

In 1735 John Wesley went as a missionary to the colony of Georgia. He was to be a pastor to the settlers and a missionary to the Indians, but he confessed that he went to save his own soul. He bombed out as a missionary. It was a terrible experience. John Wesley returned to England.

On his trip from England to Georgia the ship had been in a storm. On board this ship were some German Pietists known as Moravians who seemed to be unaffected by the storm, singing hymns in the middle of it. When he asked them if they had been afraid they answered that they were not because they were not afraid to die.

In Georgia, Wesley met another Pietist, Augustus Spangenberg, who asked Wesley directly and pointedly if he knew Jesus Christ. When John Wesley replied that he was the Savior of the world, Spangenberg pressed to know if he had saved Wesley. To which Wesley replied that he hoped that he had died to save him. But Spangenberg wanted to know if he knew it for himself. Although he answered affirmatively to the question, Wesley was not sure in his heart.

Back in England he met yet another Pietist who listened to his spiritual problem then advised him to preach faith until he had it, then because he had it, he would preach faith.

But on the evening of May 24, 1738, Wesley went to a society that met on Aldersgate Street in London where someone was reading from Luther's preface to the Epistle to the Romans. He recorded that it was about a quarter before nine, while the reader was describing the change which God works in the heart through faith in Christ, that he felt his heart strangely warmed. He felt that he did trust Christ, and Christ alone for salvation. With that he had the assurance that Christ had taken away his sins and had saved him from the law of sin and death. And the rest is history.

Wesley felt his heart strangely warmed. He was given a new heart by God through his faith in Jesus Christ. He was delivered. God can deliver you, too.

The familiar chorus says, "It's me, It's me, It's me, O Lord, Standing in the need of prayer." Grammar notwithstanding, it is indeed I who stand in the need of Christ. Where is the need? It is right here in the human heart. And deliverance is right here at the hand of God.

5
Whatever Became of Sin?

Ephesians 2:1-10

On a sunny day in September 1972, a stern-faced, plain-ly-dressed man could be seen standing still on a street corner in the busy Chicago Loop. As pedestrians hurried by on their way to lunch or business, he would solemnly lift his right arm and, pointing to the person nearest him, intone loudly the single word *GUILTY!* Then, without any change of expression, he would resume his still stance for a few moments before repeating the gesture. Then, again, the inexorable raising of his arm, the pointing, and the solemn pronouncing of the one word *GUILTY!*

The effect of this strange accusation pantomime on the passing strangers was extraordinary, almost eerie. They would stare at him, hesitate, look away, look at each other, and then at him again; then hurriedly continue on their way. One man, turning to another who was the informant of Karl Menninger who told the story in *Whatever Became of Sin?* exclaimed: "But how did *he* know?" No doubt many others had similar thoughts.

How *did* he know, indeed? If he were a student of the Bible he would have known from the biblical witness, "All have sinned, and come short of the glory of God" (Rom. 3:23).

If he were an astute observer of human nature he would have known from his observation. Obviously, something is wrong at the very core of people.

The world-famous psychiatrist, Dr. Karl Menninger, published a book in 1973 entitled *Whatever Became of*

Sin? Dr. Menninger argued that there is value in the use of both the concept of sin and the word *sin.* He said that the disappearance of the word *sin* involved a shift in the allocation of responsibility for evil. He called for the revival or reassertion of personal responsibility in all human acts, good and evil.

This is exactly where the Bible focuses on sin. Sin shows the personal responsibility of the individual for his or her acts and for his or her life. If you have personally chosen to resist God and to live your own way, the results will be disastrous.

I want to borrow Dr. Menninger's question, "Whatever became of sin?" and look at it from the biblical perspective of Ephesians 2:1-10, that tremendous passage that expresses so well what has happened to us through faith.

Whatever Became of Sin?
Some Have Tried to Explain It Away

We are well aware of the attempts to explain our bad behavior by anything but sin. Menninger took issue with this. He wrote that he believed there is "sin" which is expressed in ways which cannot be subsumed under verbal artifacts such as "crime," disease," "delinquency," "deviancy." He observed that there *is* immorality; there *is* unethical behavior; there *is* wrongdoing. And there *is* usefulness in retaining the concept, and indeed the word, *sin.* What he had in mind was behavior which pained or harmed or destroyed his neighbor or himself.

With that as a background, notice what Paul said about the nature of sin in Ephesians 2:1-3.

Notice, first, what sin is.

Some have made a distinction between the *root* sin, that principle of sin within our lives, and the *fruit* sin, those acts of sin that we commit.

The root sin is that rebellion against God, living for self. It is from the root sin that the fruit sins result. The word *sin* means missing the mark.

One time while living in Louisiana, I sneaked across the state line for a few days of deer hunting in Texas. All of my deer hunting life I had wanted to hunt deer in Texas. That was my first opportunity. We had a good trip and a fine hunt. But I did not get a deer. Here's why.

By the last morning's hunt I had seen many deer, but no bucks. My hunt was down to its last thirty minutes. In only thirty minutes they would come to pick me up and then we would return home. That morning I had seen two pairs of deer, both a doe and her yearling. By that time I was beginning to think I was not going to see a buck at all. The hunt would end and I wouldn't even get to fire my rifle. I had even propped my rifle in the corner of the deer stand.

Suddenly there appeared six deer right in front of me. I put the glasses on them and couldn't find a sign of a horn in the bunch. Then I just swept the glasses around and discovered that a buck was following them about forty yards behind. I put down the glasses. I picked up my rifle. I sighted the deer in the scope. I squeezed the trigger. The deer turned and bounded off into the trees.

I still don't understand it. I have gone over the whole thing a thousand times and I still don't know what I did wrong. Apparently I just missed that deer. I walked in increasing arcs for a long way thinking that perhaps he had run a little way then fallen over dead. But I never did find that deer. Sin is missing the mark.

The fruit sins are the expressions of sins in our lives, those sinful acts. The root sin is the sin principle that is in our lives. Resulting from this sin principle are the fruit sins, the observable sins.

Fred Fisher told this story in his book *Falling Walls: The Doctrine of Reconciliation.*

While he was pastor of a village church he was returning from a nearby city with his family. He stopped to pick up a hitch-hiker. When the man entered the car, he stank to high heaven. He had been in jail for three days for drunkenness; the stench of his vomit and the jail reeked on him.

Fisher told him that he was the pastor of the First Baptist Church in the little town where they were going.

The man then said that he was glad to know him. He was one of his church members. And he really was.

As they drove along and talked, the man promised to mend his ways and begin coming to church.

Then he said, "Pastor, I feel sorry for you. You have some of the meanest people in the world in your church."

Fisher thought he meant himself, but he did not. He was talking about one of the deacons in the church.

That afternoon, Fisher visited the shop which was owned and operated by that deacon. The deacon remarked that he saw that the pastor had met old John. Then he added that he was the meanest man in town.

Fisher observed that he found out later they were both right. They were just mean in different ways. Each thought his way of sinning was not really sinful.

Now observe what sin does.

Sin kills. Sin kills innocence, ideals, the will, self-respect, the desire to do right. Paul described us as "dead in sins and trespasses." That person who is spiritually insensitive to the promptings of the Holy Spirit and the call of Christ is dead to spiritual realities. The state is spiritual death. The reason is the control of his life by sin.

Sin controls. The person is controlled by Satan, controlled by lusts, drives, desires. Many people talk of the freedom and liberty that they have in life without Christ. Forsaking Christian principles, they will even call themselves liberated. But that is not true. They are the most controlled persons there are. Their life-style, patterns of life, and habits of sin control them. They are controlled rather than controlling their own lives.

Sin condemns. The expression, "children of wrath," means objects of God's wrath. God's wrath is not capricious. It is consistent with his character. The wrath of God is God's constant and consistent opposition to sin. God has always condemned sin. Sin has never been lightly regarded by God. From the very beginning of humanity's experience God has spoken a condemnatory word against sin.

This, then, is the picture of sin in the human life. It is hardly a pretty picture. Paul was the realist. Try as you might, sin cannot be explained away. There is something that is wrong at the very heart of mankind's existence. That wrong, expressed in both attitude and action, is sin.

Whatever Became of Sin?
Christ Has Come to Expunge It Away

After the tragic and terrible description of verses 1-3 Paul began verse 4 with these words, "But God." Something can become of our sin. It can be expunged, erased, washed away. But it is done by God's grace, not our explanation.

It is expressed in Ephesians 2:4-10. As the previous verses told what had happened tragically in humanity's experience because of sin, these verses express what terrifically has happened in our experience because of Christ. Christ has come to expunge away our sin!

God's part is seen. God's part was in sending His Son, Jesus Christ, to die for our sins.

It was rooted in God's mercy. Because God loved us He sent Jesus to die for us. Grace plays the leading role here. Jesus did not come to reveal God and to redeem mankind because we deserved it or had earned it. He came out of grace.

We always have a dog around our house. Our family is never complete unless it includes a canine of some description (or often of no adequate description).

Shortly before we moved from Natchitoches, Louisiana, to Alexandria, Louisiana, where I served with the Louisiana Baptist Convention, we had to give our dog away. Since we lived in an apartment for the first three-and-a-half months, that turned out to have been fortuitous. Not only were dogs not allowed in the apartment, but Bugger Bear was definitely not cut out for apartment living. In fact, his wandering ways was one factor that caused us to have to find another home for him.

Three days and three rains after we moved into our new house, unsodded yard and all, the children saw an article in the newspaper about the dog pound. So they sallied forth to the pound one rainy afternoon to see the dogs. Thinking they had no money their mother felt it was safe to allow them to go—just to look.

What their mother did not know was that they had tapped the lunch money fund. In a short while they returned carrying with them the cutest big-eyed, big-eared, and big-footed tawny little pooch you will ever hope to see. Supposedly about six weeks of age, he also was supposedly half-cocker spaniel and half-beagle hound. That has yet to be proved.

Of course, it didn't take but a few minutes for the dog to wiggle his way into our hearts. Tim became a solid and established member of the family.

One cold evening Tim was in the house before the fireplace playing with the children. As I watched him play, giving and receiving affection and personal attention, I thought of how fortunate Tim was. But for one choice he could still have been in the animal shelter on a cold, wet floor with no personal attention or affection. Life could have been bleak and cold and unpromising for him. Instead it was warm and bright and filled with love.

Then my thoughts moved a step further. This is the very meaning of grace. But for one choice we would be unforgiven, untouched by love, and unaware of our acceptance. God did choose us, however. And through His choice He has showed us His love through Christ, given us forgiveness of our sins, and accepted us into His family of faith.

Jesus reminded His disciples one time, "Ye have not chosen me, but I have chosen you" (John 15:16). And Paul asserted that God had chosen us as His people before the very foundation of the world (Eph. 1:4).

Grace means that God has chosen us for salvation and life even though we neither earned it nor deserved it. We can accept Him and enjoy living in faith for Him.

God has done His part. Jesus Christ has died on the cross for our sins. The "exceeding riches of his grace" have been made known to us. Salvation is God's great gift to us.

Our part, then, is to respond to this grace. "For by grace are ye saved," that is God's part; "through faith," that is our part.

We have to accept the gift that God has provided. Salvation is available for us. God has provided it. But we must respond with faith. All that God has in store for us in the forgiveness of our sins can be experienced when we turn to Him by faith and look to Jesus for salvation.

Charles H. Spurgeon never tired of telling the story of how he was saved. He had been trying to save himself by his own works. Then one snowy Sunday morning he wandered into a little chapel and sat down with the few worshipers who were there. The pastor did not show up due to the snow and the sermon was preached by a lay minister who was quite obviously a working man with limited education. That morning the minister preached on the text, "Look unto me, and be ye saved, all the ends of the earth" (Isa. 45:22). At the close of his sermon, after he repeated all that he knew to say about the text, he pointed his long, bony finger at young Spurgeon and said, "Young man, you look miserable. Look! Look unto him, young man! Look unto Jesus, and you will be saved." That morning Spurgeon looked unto Jesus and was saved.

Whatever became of your sin? It can be forgiven and forgotten by God's grace and your acceptance of Christ.

It can never be explained away. The powers of explanation never reach quite that far. But it can be expunged away. By God's grace sin can be forgiven when any person turns to Christ in faith.

6
How to Get a New You

Titus 3:3-7

Presbyterian pastor James W. Angell in his book *Yes Is a World* tells of walking one night along the beach in Santa Barbara, California. In that city of blue and creamy charm he stopped in the midst of his walk in front of a wig shop. A sign caught his eye through the lighted front window. The sign proclaimed: "Buy yourself a wig—it's the quickest way to create a new 'you.'"

If a wig can make you feel that way about yourself perhaps you ought to buy one. With a new wig one may be able to have a better self-image of oneself. Or perhaps a wig would improve one's self-concept. With a better self-image and a better self-concept it just might be that a person would feel reborn, that there was a new you. A better way, however, to get a new you would be to receive that salvation God offers through Jesus Christ. Through a new birth you receive a new you.

Titus is known as one of the Pastoral Epistles. It is generally believed that it was written by Paul to Titus, a younger minister who had been given a responsible ministering task. Both in form and in content the letter to Titus resembles strongly the two letters to Timothy with which it is joined as a Pastoral Epistle. As a Pastoral Epistle it is filled with instruction and information to guide a fledgling pastor in his ministry.

The third chapter begins with suggestions about how they were to relate to the ruling authorities. It moves very quickly, though, from rulers to all persons. Then, in a brief passage it gives a very complete statement about the meaning of salvation. It may have been a part of an old confessional statement as seen by the closing statement with which verse 8 begins, "This is a faithful saying." That faithful saying, or "The saying is true" as the Revised Standard Version renders it, is a good summary statement of the meaning of salvation. It tells what it means to be completely changed through salvation, to be born anew through faith in Jesus Christ.

How do you get a new you? Maybe you can get a new you through buying a new wig. But the better way would be through what Jesus described to Nicodemus in John 3 as the new birth. Only when you have been remade through faith in Christ can you have a new you. Two significant questions immediately come to mind.

The first question is:

Why Do You Need a New You? In a Word, Because of Sin.

The first question that presents itself to us is: "Why do you need a new you?" The answer to that question in a word is: because of sin.

Paul was fond of making contrasts between sin and salvation. In more than one place in the writings of Paul we run across "before" and "after" statements that contrast life before salvation with life after salvation. One of those places is in Titus 3:3. Here he presents what the person is who is lost in sin. It is expressed in the words, "For we ourselves were once . . ." (RSV). That is what the Christian was before that person experienced salvation through faith in Jesus Christ.

Sin is due to missing the mark. The basic meaning of the word commonly translated *sin* in the New Testament is missing the mark. In its simplest form then, sin is missing the mark of what God expects us to be and enables us to be. I once read of a mountaineer who had a great reputation as a marksman. Whoever followed him found target rings on trees, fences, and barn doors with a bullet hole in the center. When he was asked to explain the secret of his skill he answered that it was easy. He just shot then drew the circle around the hole. Anyone can hit the mark that way. But in life it is not quite that simple. God has set before us a mark of what life should be. By our sin we have missed that mark. In our lives there is this principle of sin that causes us to keep doing things that miss the mark.

But how do you describe sin? Notice that Paul showed several ways in which sin manifests itself. We can begin to form a description of our sin and thus gain an understanding of the sin in our lives.

Sin is foolish. The first descriptive word is "foolish." Sin is just foolish. So much of sin is more foolish than it is bad. How foolish it is for persons to continue practices in their lives that are self-destructive and self-defeating. How foolish it is for a person to think that the results of sin apply to everyone but him. The surgeon general of the United States has placed warnings on all cigarette packages of the possible danger to human life through the continued practice of smoking cigarettes. But people persist in buying and smoking cigarettes. And preachers keep on burying people who died of lung cancer. It is foolish for us to miss God's mark by purposely carrying out self-destructive activities. Morally and spiritually, as well as physically, people act foolishly.

Sin is disobedience. We miss God's mark when we are disobedient to God. God has revealed to us what He expects of us. A person should not really have to stop and think about whether to steal, lie, or commit adultery. God has already expressed Himself on those things pretty clearly in the Ten Commandments. And one should not have to ponder long about whether life should be lived in obedience to God or rebellion against God. The evidence is in that it is better to be obedient. But sin is disobedience. I heard of a little boy who would walk across the street to his grandmother's house just to say no. Often we will go to greater lengths to be disobedient than to be obedient to the revealed will of God.

Sin is deceptive. The King James Version translates this third word "deceived" while the Revised Standard Version uses the term "led astray." From the very beginning of the human experience with sin, as seen in Genesis 3, the nature of sin has been deception. The tempter deceived Eve, and Eve deceived Adam, and both of them deceived themselves. But none of them were able to deceive God. Sin is deceptive in its allure and in its promises. But God is neither deceived nor mocked. And a person does reap what has been sown in the suffering and effects of sin on human life.

Sin is enslaving. In the fourth manifestation of sin, persons are described as "slaves to various passions and pleasures" (RSV). Interestingly enough, the very persons who proclaim their freedom most loudly and persistently are the most hopelessly enslaved. When a person can no longer make a free choice but is compelled to a certain action or pattern of behavior that person is no longer free. That person is a slave to personal passions. There are some people who would really desire to make a change in their life-style or in some of their activities. But because of a reputation to uphold or an image to enhance they feel that they cannot. That person is a slave. Others may marvel at the freedom from conventional ways of behavior they have; but they hear the rattle of their chains.

Sin fills with malice and envy. The person who is caught up in sin lives life with malice and envy toward others. Malice is that general ill will that one bears toward another. Envy is that spirit that one carries in the heart against another person. Perhaps someone else has received the promotion you thought was yours, or won the beauty title you thought you had clinched, or got the recognition that you felt you had earned by your hard work. In the end, you might congratulate that person upon the recognition or achievement. Publicly, you might say that the best person won. But that first reaction you felt and that feeling that you carry deep within your heart might well be envy toward that person. Whereas the Spirit of Christ calls us to love other people and to desire their best good, the spirit of envy often eats away at the human heart.

Sin causes hate. The last way that Paul described sin in Titus 3:3 has to do with hate: ". . . hated by men and hating one another" (RSV). How terrible that sounds! A life that is filled with hate and that both gives and receives hate does not sound very appealing. But that is exactly the way Paul described the manifestation of sin in our lives. During the Watergate scandal that ultimately led to the resignation of Richard M. Nixon from the presidency of the United States, the nation was shocked to learn that the President of our country kept an enemies list. I don't know why it shocked us so much, except that it demonstrated a behavior and an attitude that we thought was beneath the dignity of a President. In fact, many of us carry around private little enemies lists and hate lists. They may never be publicly displayed. The names may never be written down in a formal list. But many of us carry in our hearts our own personal enemies list. That is a result of sin in our lives. God would much desire that we make out a love list than an enemies list.

But notice that these things lumped together by the apostle Paul in this passage are not necessarily the gross things that we often describe as sin. They can grow to it. And the gross things can result from them. We can identify with William Temple who once remarked that his sins were not scarlet but gray, all gray. The gray sins, however, are no less sins. They show very clearly why we need salvation.

A hundred years or so ago when he was in a cynical mood, Mark Twain wrote a story called "The Great Catastrophe." Before he had finished the story he had worked the characters into such a predicament that no matter what they did they would end up losing. He closed the story by saying that he had those people in such a fix that he could not get them out. Anyone who thought he could was welcome to try.

Indeed, through our sin we have ourselves in such fixes that we cannot get ourselves out of them. We need outside help. We need divine help. We need a new birth. That is why you need a new you. It is because of your sin.

But to the next question:

How Do You Get a New You? In a Word, Because of Salvation

If the first question is: "Why do you need a new you?" and the answer to that in a word is because of your sin— then the second question is: "How do you get a new you?" —and the answer to that, in a word, is because of salvation.

Verse 3 begins the contrast of how we were without Christ. Verse 4 completes the contrast and tells how it happens. Verse 3 began with the words, "For we ourselves were once . . ." and then moves on to complete the contrast in verse 4 and the opening words of verse 5 with the statement, "but when the goodness and loving kindness of God our Savior appeared, he saved us" (RSV). Our salvation is due to the goodness and loving kindness of God.

Salvation is the experience that one has with God. It is the inclusive term. That salvation that we experience through faith in God through Jesus Christ is then described in various terms. But the inclusive term for it is salvation.

Salvation is regeneration. The word *regeneration* means making new. And that is exactly what God has done for us in Jesus Christ. He has made us new. There is a cleansing of the person, the life, the heart that comes about through faith in Jesus Christ. And the result of that cleansing is that we have been made new, born again, regenerated in Jesus Christ.

William Temple once observed that there is no way that he could write a play like Shakespeare's plays. If one were to have given him the play and told him to write one like that he could never do it. But if the spirit of Shakespeare could some way come into his life and live in it then he could write plays like that. He then observed that there is no way that one could set before him the life of Christ and tell him to live a life like that. He could not do it. But if the Spirit of Christ were to come to live in him then he could live that life. Through regeneration that is what happens. The Spirit of Christ comes to live in the newborn Christian and he can begin to live a new kind of life, a Christ-kind of life.

Salvation is renewal. Another way that salvation is described in verse 4 is as a renewal of the Holy Spirit. The greatest kind of renewal is not the urban renewal that comes from buying deteriorated property in downtown areas of cities and removing it so that new areas can be created. It is not the refurbishing of blighted buildings. The greatest renewal is the refurbishing and reclamation of blighted and deteriorated lives. God does that through Jesus Christ. That comes about through the renewal of the Holy Spirit in the human heart. This Holy Spirit is richly poured out on believers through Jesus Christ, as expressed in verse 6.

Salvation has definite results. When you have experienced salvation there are some results that will begin to show up in your life. You can know that something significant has happened.

The first result is a past reference. Sin is forgiven. That forgiveness is indicated in verse 7 with the term "justified by his grace." When you have been justified, you have been forgiven. Someone has expressed it by saying that it is "just-as-if-I'd" never sinned. Justification comes about through the grace of God in Jesus Christ. Jesus forgives us. That makes us just in the sight of God. The sins of the past no longer have to be considered. In Christ one is justified. The sins are forgiven.

There is also a present reference to the results of salvation. Christians are heirs of God. They become the children of God. There is a completely new quality of life available to the individual. When you are an heir, you have a claim to inherit all that is available. As heirs of God we can fall heir to the greatness and the grace of God. The children of Vietnam who were brought to the United States during the war in Southeast Asia were adopted into American homes. Before they had known terror, devastation, and poverty. But with the adoption into an American home they had an entirely new quality of life. They had freedom, and provision, and hope. That is all included in the new quality of life that we have through faith in Jesus Christ. Adoption is another of the terms used to describe salvation. When you are adopted into a family, you become an heir. As heirs of God we are recipients of the riches of His grace. That present reality can be experienced now.

But a third result of salvation that is presented is future —the "hope of eternal life." We usually think of eternal life in quantitative terms. It is a life that goes on and on. It is a life that lasts forever. That is true, but eternal life also has a qualitative side to it. It is a life that is fit for eternity. Eternity in the presence of God may seem more like punishment than reward to some people. But eternal life is the hope of the Christian. And it is not so much reward as where the road with God leads. It is the end result of having expressed faith in God through Jesus Christ and having experienced salvation. Because of that the believer has eternal life. It is a life that is fit to live with God eternally.

Why do you need a new you? You need a new you because of your sin. How do you get a new you? You get a new you because of your salvation through faith in Jesus Christ.

It is not too much to hope that you can have a new you. The new you can actually happen. Do you need proof? Then observe this story as told by Ernest Gordon and Peter Funk in their book *Guidebook for the New Christian.*

W. A. Haberern was an insurance agent who consistently witnessed for Christ in his own quiet way. An important element in his witnessing was his church which was extremely active in helping new Christians grow in their faith. During a rainstorm he took shelter under a storefront awning. A young man and a young woman scurried in beside him. There was something about their appearance that touched him. Their blue jeans were old and the rest of their clothing was in poor shape. They both looked tired and unhealthy.

He introduced himself to them and then invited them to a Bible study class. They said they would come. Of course, they did not. Several days later he saw them on the street. Again he quietly suggested that they would be welcome at the Bible study. They did not appear. A third time he met them by chance. Once more he invited them to the Bible study. That time they came. From that moment their life-style began to change.

Rick and Jenny had lived a sordid life. Completely without money, Rick had sold his wife to another man so they could have a place to stay. Drugs took whatever money they had. On welfare, they were both emotionally and physically sick. At the age of eighteen Jenny had lost most of her teeth. The welfare department gave them up, observing that they were hopeless and would doubtlessly be on welfare the rest of their lives.

But government bureaucracy had not reckoned with the power of Christ. Jenny and Rick were both converted to Christ. To the amazement of everyone except the people of the church, Rick found a good job and held it. They got a pleasant apartment instead of their old hotel. Both began witnessing to others and bringing their friends to church. It took almost six months for all of this to happen. But a complete transformation of their lives had taken place.

You can get a new you. It comes through faith in Jesus Christ. You need a new you because of your sin. You can get a new you because of salvation. You can be a new person. Christ can give new life. Why don't you accept Christ as your Savior and get a new you?

7
Your Search

Luke 15:11-24

One of the finest stories of King Arthur and the knights of the Round Table is the story of the search for the Holy Grail. On the day when Sir Galahad was introduced to the Round Table, a day which was the 454th anniversary of the Feast of the Pentecost, the Holy Grail appeared to the knights. The Holy Grail was supposed to be the cup from which the Lord drank wine at the Last Supper. It had been carried to England but had disappeared when the keepers became unpure. Upon seeing this sight, Sir Gawain pledged that he would search for a year and a day to find the Holy Grail. Whereupon all the other knights made the same pledge. So began the search. And so came the adventures. As each knight searched for this Holy Grail he had many great and exciting adventures. It was Sir Galahad in company with Sir Percival and Sir Bors who found the Holy Grail. Galahad was able to find the Grail because he was pure and spotless in his character.

This is an ancient story of a search that leads to many places and through many adventures. It is a search for an elusive object. All of those who searched for it had some vision of what they were trying to find but it was never too clear in their minds.

There is no better way to characterize this generation than by its ceaseless, endless searching. Look at the dissatisfaction, note the restlessness, watch the almost-frantic running from one fad and interest to another. It would seem that the people of this day are frantically searching for something. And the great problem is that this search is not well-defined. There is something that is missing, something that each wants, but what it is for sure no one seems to know. The knights of the Round Table searched for the Holy Grail. Perhaps the reason our search seems so futile is that it is for personal gain, or selfish satisfaction for the most part.

As a character to speak to our age in this endless, frantic search, none stands out quite so well as this one whom we have labeled the prodigal son. His search, so much like today's search, led him from the love and comfort of his father's home to the far country; from a life of usefulness and worth to the lowest of degradation and vileness, from a character of popularity and brilliance to a beaten, miserable whelp, from a fine standard of living to riotous living.

As with all of Jesus' stories, this was told for a purpose. In verse 2 we are told that the scribes and Pharisees were murmuring that Jesus "receiveth sinners, and eateth with them." And Jesus told these three related stories found in the fifteenth chapter of Luke—the lost sheep, the lost coin, and the lost boy—to prove to them that the Son of Man came to seek and to save sinners. In His effort to find and restore the lost He was showing the heart of God. This has always been God's interest—to restore to fellowship those who have been removed from that fellowship.

It is evident that the prodigal son was not in fellowship with the father. And it was due to his search. He felt that there were things he wanted and deserved and he determined to search them out. Elements of the search of the prodigal son can be seen in the search of people of today.

A Search for Freedom

The first thing seen in even a cursory reading of this parable is that the young man wanted his freedom. He had begun to chafe under the discipline of his father. He felt that he was missing all of the meaningful, exciting things of life. He felt that he was being cheated of experiences that every growing boy ought to have.

These are contemporary thoughts. There are more than a few children of all ages who now think that discipline, rather than helping shape character, is hindering their free movement. They think admonitions about keeping their lives clean are cheating them of experiences that are needed to make life meaningful and free.

All of this is based on a misconception of the meaning of freedom. For the young man freedom meant to be able to do what he wanted to do. For the father freedom meant that he should become what he ought to be. And there is a tremendous difference in the two thoughts. For most people today the thoughts of freedom are the thoughts of unrestrained desire. The desire and greed of this young man is quickly seen. His father gave him his portion, which, if there were only two sons as the story seems to indicate, would be a third of the estate. He immediately turned it into cash and went on his way. He was going to be free! He was going to live! He was going to have a high-heeled good time on his new-found wealth which had no strings attached!

But where does this type of freedom lead? Look at the son again. He has been free. He has done what he wanted to. Look at him, how free he is! This is what he thought when he left. This is what it looked like from the outside.

But what is it like from the inside? He is not free. He is bound! He has to do these things! All of this time he has been diverting himself with his activities. As Helmut Thielicke has said:

> He cannot be alone; he must have diversion. And one day this realization must have struck the prodigal son too. ... But when he *cannot* and therefore *must*, then he is no longer free! No, God knows, he is not free. This is the great

new thing that suddenly dawns upon him—him who, after all, set out to be free, free above all from his father.

He is *bound* to his homesickness, so he *must* amuse himself.

He is *bound* to urges, so he *must* satisfy them.

He is *bound* to a grand style of living and therefore he *cannot* let it go. He would be prepared to lie and cheat and disregard every good resolution, so spellbound is he by his standards of living.

That's what freedom looks like outside the Father's house—to be *bound,* to *have* to do this and that, to be under a *spell,* to be *compelled* to pursue the path he has chosen by an inexorable law.

Others can talk about his sophistication and his freedom. Only he hears the rattle of the invisible chains in which he walks and they are beginning to make him groan.[1]

This type of freedom separates one from the source and origin of his blessings. All the time that he was living it up, all the time his substance was being spent on riotous living, he was using the blessings of the father without taking him into account. His body, possessions, money, clothes, shoes, food, drink, all came from his father. In themselves they are good things; otherwise the father would not have given them to him. But as he uses them they are his undoing, for he uses them for himself, he uses them *without* the father.

And this is our situation. In getting free we have taken great pride in our scientific advance, our medical skill, in our refrigerators, freezers, computers, cars, our houses and buildings, and have not stopped to think that all blessings—spiritual and physical—come from God. We sing "Praise God, from whom all blessings flow" on Sunday morning. But on Sunday afternoon the blessings are used without any thought of God. How far can we go in our freedom? Can you not see, that in renouncing God and his claim on your life, you are renouncing the source of all that you count worthwhile?

This type of freedom eventually leads to the "far country." Where is the far country? Dr. C. Roy Angell quotes Ellis A. Fuller as saying: "It is anywhere that a man tries to live without God." He then added:

> It can be the most beautiful city in America; it can be the most beautiful home in your city. I used to think of the far country in the words of Kipling, "Where the trails run out and stop." I used to think it was some wild western frontier town where the mud or dust was deep in the streets, where there was no paint on the houses, where the outlaws lived, and men killed each other for nothing. I used to think it was in the town in nowhere that was filled with the scum of the earth, where saloons and bawdy houses were the only hangouts men had, but alas, I realize that a man can be in a far country in the house that is next to mine, where the church bells peal out every Sunday. But the far country is just as Dr. Fuller said anywhere, anywhere that a man tries to live without God.[2]

Do you want freedom? Is your search the search for freedom? It comes by giving yourself to Christ and following His will, not by giving free rein to your own wants and desires.

A Search for Meaning

And so freedom has gone its way. When the prodigal looked at himself in the pigpen he knew that his freedom was not real freedom at all. He was bound to his actions, a slave to his sin.

And now there came another significant search—the search for meaning. He was faced with what the late Paul Tillich identified as the root of the anxiety of our time—the loss of the meaning of life.

His whole life had been wrapped up in his freedom. But now that bubble had burst. A famine had come. His easy money had played out. His newfound friends had deserted him. He could not even get a job. The fact that he "joined himself to a citizen of that country" proves that he was not given a regular job but rather took up with the man. And he was put to feeding the hogs. To a Jew, and this story was told to Jews, there could be nothing more degrading. And in this situation he began to examine himself, he looked deeply within his soul, he carefully surveyed his life. He was trying to find meaning to this life.

Meaning is found in repentance. When he began to look at himself as he really was and to consider the blessings that even the hired servants of his father had, he repented of his sin. "And when he came to himself . . . ." How this describes us in our sin and rebellion against God. We are actually beside ourselves in thinking that we are the masters of our own destiny. He came to himself after realizing his true condition; after coming to his true self.

This is one of the basic steps of repentance. We cannot repent and turn to God until we realize that we need to repent. As long as we think that we have no sin, or that we are living as well as the next person, repentance will not come. What we must do, is to see ourselves as God sees us—sinners who have rebelled against God and thwarted His will before our own desires.

Another important element of repentance is to see the need of God's mercy. We are told that "no man gave unto him" and also that "I perish with hunger!" He was at the end of his resources, perishing with hunger, no man giving to him either love or food, there was no place he could turn but to his father.

And this is where we find ourselves. We are thrust to Christ. We find that our good resolutions, the counsel of our friends, our well-meaning acts do not fill the hunger of the soul. No one can give to us what we so desperately need—salvation comes only from the Father. And this is available when we repent and turn to Him.

Also involved in repentance is the decision of will leading to action. "I will arise and go to my father," the young man stated. This is the proof of real repentance. Just seeing yourself as you are, just realizing that you are at the end of your resources, could very well lead to remorse or despair. But now there is a decision of will that leads to action. The proof of repentance is when you do something about it, you arise and go to your Father.

In the search for meaning to life there is a return. The search for meaning is found in repentance, and then there is a return—a return to God, to favor, to usefulness. And you say, "Well, that makes the story all right. He has sowed his wild oats. He has had his good time. And now he has returned." Doesn't the Bible say, "Train up a child in the way he should go: and when he is old, he will not depart from it?" This just bears out Scripture.

Yes, he returned. But there is one very significant fact that is often overlooked. He returned, but he did not return the way he left. There is something radically different about him now. Oh, surely he left in pomp and self-confidence and now he is returning in rags and degradation. But there is more than just the way he looks, something has happened within his life that can never be removed. He can be forgiven but the marks of his sin cannot be erased. And that is one thing that we often forget about our sin. Even after repentance and return, even after forgiveness, the marks of sin are indelibly etched in our hearts and lives. These things cannot just be forgiven and forgotten. In our experience and in our lives there are hurts and scars that forever remain. And the tragedy of it is that it is so unnecessary. Those marks did not have to be there.

Omar Khayyam expressed it for us:

> The Moving Finger writes;
> And having writ,
> Moves on;
> Nor all your Piety nor wit shall lure it back,
> To cancel half a line,
> Nor all your Tears wash out a word of it.

A Search for Acceptance

And so the young man known as the prodigal made a search for freedom and found only the bondage of sin. He made a search for meaning to life and ended in repentance. And he started the long road back to home. And in this journey we see yet another search—the search for acceptance. This is one of our greatest needs, to be accepted: to be accepted by our family, to be accepted by our friends, to be accepted by our crowd, and most important, to be accepted by our God.

Many of the things that people do they do, not because they necessarily want to do them, but in order that they will be accepted by their group. And this could very well have been true in the experience of the prodigal. He didn't leave home to be a rascal, but in the fast company in which he found himself he had to do some of these things to be accepted.

Now the acceptance he sought was of a different order and actually more important to him. He wanted to be accepted by his father. He even made up a little speech about it. He knew exactly what he would say when he first met his father.

And this gets us to the real point of the story. The story is not about the prodigal son as much as it is about the loving, waiting father. You remember the criticism of the scribes and Pharisees. Jesus used this story for two purposes: to justify his own mission in the teeth of his critics; and to rebuke the scribes and Pharisees. He was showing them that God was like the waiting father. God is like the father who sought out his lost son, and waited for him to return to his fellowship.

This is not just any father, this is God. A.M. Hunter in *Interpreting the Parables* told the story of a certain prodigal son who, on turning up in "the far country" of another parish, was advised by the minister there to go home and "his father would kill the fatted calf for him." The prodigal obeyed. Months later he met the same minister again and was asked, hopefully: "Well, and did he kill the fatted calf for you?" "No," came the rueful reply, "But he nearly killed the prodigal son!"

What Jesus does in this parable is to state the fundamental principle of God's dealing with sinners, and thereby justify His own loving concern for them. What we are entitled to learn from the parable is that God loves the sinner before he repents, and that, when he does repent, God forgives him and restores him to His great family.

This is acceptance of the first magnitude. It is against God that we have sinned. It is God whom we have rebuked. It is God to whom we have turned our backs and resolved to go our own ways. And now He comes to forgive us of our sin and restore us to fellowship with Him.

And what forgiveness and acceptance it is! The boy could not even finish his prepared speech. The father interrupted him. He ordered for him a robe which showed honor, a ring which showed authority, and shoes which showed sonship. On top of all this he ordered the fatted calf killed and feasting and merriment because one who was dead to him had been restored to life and usefulness.

Remember? Paul said in Ephesians that we had been dead in our sins and trespasses. This father was waiting for the boy to return. When he was a great way off his father saw him, had compassion on him, and ran to meet him. He was looking for him to return. We are dead and apart from God due to our sin. We need to see ourselves and repent and turn to God.

Will He welcome us? As the father was looking for the boy so God is even now actively searching your heart and calling you to Him. That might be that uneasiness you feel. That might be the restlessness you experience at night. That might be the constant urging your very soul experiences. And you come to God—even with your sin— you ask His forgiveness, pledge your life to Him, commit yourself to Him, and He accepts you as you are and restores you to fellowship and blessedness.

Are you looking for acceptance? You can find it in God. William Barclay related that once Lincoln was asked how he was going to treat the rebellious Southerners when they had finally been defeated and had returned to the Union. The questioner expected that Lincoln would take a dire vengeance, but he answered that he would treat them as if they had never been away. It is the wonder of the love of God that God treats us like that.

That is your search. Are you searching for freedom? for meaning? for acceptance? They are all found in Christ. True freedom is that freedom we find in the Lord's will. Meaning to life is only realized when the life is lived for God. Acceptance is ours and forgiveness, when we turn to God in repentance and faith. Your search can be ended when you discover Christ.

Notes

1. Helmut Thielicke, *The Waiting Father,* trans. by John W. Doberstein (New York: Harper and Brothers, 1959), p. 25.

2. C. Roy Angell, *Baskets of Silver* (Nashville: Broadman Press, 1955), pp. 32-33.

8
Explanation of an Enigma

Acts 4:13

In the presidential election year of 1976 there was one enigma that stumped the old-time, old-line political observers. That was the amazing success of Jimmy Carter of Georgia for the Democratic nomination for the presidency of the United States and ultimately his election as President of the United States.

Everything about Carter's success seemed wrong to the old pols: he was a newcomer to the political scene; he was a novice, having served only as the governor of Georgia previously; he was a Southerner—and Southerners were not supposed to have national appeal; and he was a committed, evangelical Christian.

One very interesting explanation for his appeal centered in his Christian faith. This said that his outright, frank, and unadorned confession of faith in Christ struck to the heart of evangelical Protestantism throughout the country. But they are still seeking an explanation of the enigma of Jimmy Carter's fast rise to prominence.

The Jewish authorities also sought an explanation for an enigma one day in Jerusalem. The background was the healing of the lame man at the gate of the Temple by Peter and John. Then Peter preached to the people, explaining that the man had been healed by the power of the resurrected Jesus Christ. All of this caused such a turmoil that they arrested Peter and John. After a night in jail they questioned them. Again Peter spoke. Again he attributed the deed to the power of the resurrected Christ and closed by asserting that salvation was only through Jesus Christ.

These disciples were an enigma to the Jewish authorities. Everything about them seemed wrong: they were uneducated; they had not been theologically or rabbinically trained; they were common people, fishermen.

Where did they get that kind of power? How were they able to speak like that? What enabled them to command the attention of so many of the people? What had changed their lives?

Could there be an explanation for this enigma? Yes. The explanation is found in their own observation recorded in the latter part of Acts 4:13, ". . . and they took knowledge of them, that they had been with Jesus."

This was the explanation of the enigma then.

And it is the only plausable explanation of the enigma of Christian discipleship today. How can a life be totally changed and redirected? How can untrained persons teach in Sunday School and lead in church programs? How can common folks have a spiritual power that defies rational explanation? What is the source of strength for Christian ministry to others? How can people show love and share love with persons who might not be particularly lovable? What is it that can cause regular, common people to step out in bold discipleship? There is but one explanation for this enigma: they have been with Jesus.

Discipleship is following Jesus. It begins with the commitment of life in faith to Jesus Christ. Then it continues in following Jesus throughout all of life. When people have been with Jesus then they have a spiritual power for all of life. It shows up in many ways.

A Divine Compassion

In this explanation of an enigma there is a divine compassion. Having been with Jesus, Peter and John had absorbed some of the compassion of Jesus. Looking at the lame man at the gate of the Temple with the compassion of Jesus, they were moved to heal him through the power of this same Jesus.

The man stood before them healed. Of this there could be no question. Their compassion to bring him healing had come from Jesus.

Jesus always looked on people with compassion. In any crowd he saw the faces of people with compassion. Typical is the expression of his compassion found in Matthew 9:36: "But when he saw the multitudes, he was moved with compassion on them, because they fainted, and were scattered abroad, as sheep having no shepherd."

It is only when we have been with Jesus that we can have the divine compassion for others in need. All around us people live with great need. There are the sinful and the unforgiven. And there are the alienated, the grieving, the confused, the sick, and the unfortunate.

Bill Self, pastor of the Wieuca Road Baptist Church in Atlanta, Georgia, and his wife Carolyn have written a book together entitled *A Survival Kit for the Stranded.* In the introduction they indicated that they hoped the book would provide a survival kit for the times a person might feel stranded. And the stranded people are all around us. To see them and to move to their help we will have to exercise the divine compassion toward human need that comes from having been with Jesus.

The difference in how we see people can come with being with Jesus. Bruce Larson in *The Edge of Adventure,* written with Keith Miller, tells the story of the friend in Illinois who joined a small group for prayer and Bible study that met one night a week. Although the man had come quite a way in his Christian commitment he complained each week about the customers in his store. He said that they were unfair, demanding, and always trying to take advantage of him.

After a while this man had a new experience with God. Then he began to see the people who came into his store as people sent from God, whether they came to buy a package of nails or a washing machine. He anticipated each sale as an adventure in personal relationships.

At Christmastime this man remarked to the group with amazement one night that he was surprised at how the people in that town had changed. The Christmas before they were rude, pushy, demanding, but that year he had not had a difficult customer in his store. They were all understanding people and trying their best to cooperate. Who had changed? Not the people. He had changed. He had begun to look at them with compassion and love because he had been with Jesus.

A Divine Compulsion

When you have been with Jesus there is a divine compulsion to make it known. You cannot remain silent about it. You must tell someone. Telling someone about your experiences with Jesus is called witnessing.

Not knowing what else to do with Peter and John, the Jewish authorities forbade them to preach in the name of Jesus or even to talk about Jesus. They were afraid to jail them or to beat them because of the reaction of the people to them and their deed of mercy. So they forbade them to speak any more in the name of Jesus.

Their answer to the authorities is a classic. To them Peter and John said, "Whether it be right in the sight of God to hearken unto you more than unto God, judge ye. For we cannot but speak the things which we have seen and heard" (Acts 4:19-20).

Obedience to God and the willingness to share Jesus Christ is more important than fear of others, whether the authorities or the neighbors. It was said of John Knox that he feared God so much that he never feared the face of any man. The Christian disciple who has been with Jesus fears God more than people. He has a divine compulsion to share his faith.

We think of the Baptist contribution to religious liberty in the United States in terms of this divine compulsion.

The early Baptists felt that they had to share what they had seen and heard. The dissenting preachers in Colonial Virginia were required to get a license from the authorities to preach, which many Baptists refused to do. They felt if they were licensed by King Jesus they did not need to be licensed by King George. And many of them suffered persecution because of it.

One of the most notable cases was that of James Ireland in Culpeper County, Virginia, in 1769. Soon after coming to Culpeper County he was warned to quit preaching. But after counting the cost of freedom or confinement, liberty or a prison, he determined to suffer for Christ, if necessary, since he had ventured all for Him.

Having been seized when he preached, the judge decided to make an example of him. Despite his weakness from cold and improper food he preached through the bars of the small iron gate in the jail. They hacked at his outstretched hands with swords as he preached. They whipped others outside the jail so that he could see and hear their distress as a warning of the future punishment he might receive. They uncovered a plot to blow up the jail. A physician rescued him from attempted poisoning. His tormentors burned pods of Indian pepper to smoke him to death. Yet he continued his witness and wrote letters to his friends headed, "From my palace in Culpeper." At length he was released. But he was too weak from the experiences to resume preaching with his old power.

Where do you start in your witnessing when you have the divine compulsion to tell of Christ? Right where you are. Whether in your home, your neighborhood, your class, or your job, you can begin to tell of Christ right where you are. A railroad engineer came to his pastor to ask to be put to work as a new Christian. The pastor told the engineer that there was no position in the church open at that time. But he did say that he knew of one job that only he could do. Then the preacher asked the engineer if his fireman were a Christian. That's where you start: right where you are.

A Divine Companion

The whole secret of having been with Jesus is the companionship of the Christ Himself. In this explanation of an enigma there is a divine companionship. The person who has been with Jesus is never the same because of that experience. R.E.O White once wrote that none who lingered in Jesus' presence failed to be cleansed by His company.

Jesus changes lives. The witness is given very clearly that the way to salvation is through faith in Jesus Christ. In Acts 4:12 Peter said, "Neither is there salvation in any other: for there is none other name under heaven given among men, whereby we must be saved."

Jesus still changes the lives of the persons who come to Him in faith. Leonard Griffith in *Ephesians: A Positive Affirmation* passed on the story of Meg who came to know Christ as Savior through the witness of The Church of the Saviour in Washington, D.C.

Meg came to Christ out of a life of alcoholism and prostitution. She had tried marriage for a while in the hope that it would help her, but it did not. She still crawled the gutters. Her numerous extramarital adventures drove her war veteran husband to attempted suicide and a period in a psychiatric ward.

When Meg found the love of Christ she was changed completely. She stopped drinking and swearing. Her marriage was saved. She looked out on the world with new eyes. She even went back to her old haunts and told her former companions about Jesus. Meg found that love among the people at The Church of the Saviour. They were people who accepted her and cared for her and gave themselves to her as no one had ever done before. They brought the presence of Christ into her life and they brought her into the presence of Christ. She said that at first she thought these people were crazy. Then she did not care what they were. She suddenly wanted what they had. What they had was salvation through Jesus Christ.

Jesus also charges persons. The one thing that charged these early disciples with the power and the motivation to give this kind of witness, to live this kind of life, to practice this kind of bold discipleship was the fact that they had been with Jesus.

My football playing experience was limited to play in the municipal recreation program leagues in the city where I was reared. I played center on the neighborhood football team that was entered in the 125-pound league, which meant that none of the players could weigh over 125 pounds. Our team had made it through about half the season unbeaten and untied. We were then about to meet the team that would be the toughest we had played all season. But also during that week the coach had received notice from the Marine reserves that he had been called to active duty and would have to go to Korea before the week was up. And so he made his speech to us before the game. He said something like this: "Boys, you have played real well all season and I've been very proud of you. I'm sure you all know by now that I have received my notice that I will have to be going to Korea. This will be the last game for this team that I'll coach. And it may be the last game I ever coach. You know as well as I do what is happening in Korea and that a lot of people never come back. So, boys, I'm asking you to get in there and fight and to win this one for Perry!" You never saw such an inspired bunch of little boys in your life. We went in there to win that one for Perry and win it we did.

Jesus continually charges us to get out into the world with that same kind of bold discipleship. Our greatest charge for service comes from having been in his presence.

What explanation is there for the enigma of common

people at work in the world with power and love? They have been with Jesus. This is the only explanation.

What is the explanation for changed lives, forgiven sin, a new life? It comes from having been in the presence of Jesus and the acceptance of Christ by faith.

And this is also the meaning of Christian discipleship. It is to be with Jesus. Perhaps you need to begin your pilgrimage of faith with Christ this very day. Will you give your life to Him in faith? Will you come into His presence so that your life can be changed by Him and charged by Him to real discipleship?

9
It's Dynamite!

Romans 1:16-17

How would you like to read your own obituary? One morning in 1888 Alfred B. Nobel, inventor of dynamite, the man who grew wealthy by producing weapons of destruction, awoke to read his own obituary! It seems that his brother had died, and a French reporter carelessly reported the death of the wrong brother!

Anyone would have been shaken. But to Alfred B. Nobel, the shock was overwhelming. He suddenly saw himself as others saw him—an amazing discovery that few persons make. He was to the world "the dynamite king," the industrialist who became rich from explosives. So far as the general public was concerned this was the whole story of Nobel's life. To the world he was quite simply a merchant of death, and for that alone he was remembered.

Horrified by his obituary, Nobel resolved to do something different with his life. He would will his fortune for prizes to those who have done the most for the causes in which he believed. His last will and testament would express his life's ideals. The result was the Nobel prizes, five awards granted each year, the most notable of which is the peace prize, one of the most valued prizes granted today.

When Nobel, the Swedish chemist, invented dynamite he gave it a name taken from the Greek word that means *power*. That is the very word that Paul used to describe the gospel in Romans 1:16.

88

Romans 1:16-17 expresses the theme of the Book of Romans: the righteousness of God.

But how do you describe God's righteousness? Righteousness means right standing. And that is good news, that we can have right standing with God. And that good news has power. Paul had seen that power at work throughout the Roman world. He wanted to tell the Roman Christians about it. And in the process he has left us a rich repository of truth about the righteousness of God.

We have in our hands a gospel, the good news that we can have right standing with God. It is dynamite!

Affirmation

When you think of the gospel as dynamite you make an affirmation. Paul said, "I am not ashamed of the gospel." That sounds a bit negative to us. What he meant was that he was proud of the gospel. "I have complete confidence in the gospel" is the way the *Good News Bible* translates it.

It is an amazing thing to think of the background of that statement. Paul had been imprisoned in Philippi, chased out of Thessalonica, stoned in Lystra, smuggled out of Berea, laughed at in Athens. He had preached in Corinth where his message was foolishness to the Greeks and a stumbling block to the Jews, and out of that background Paul declared that he was proud of the gospel. There was something in the gospel which made Paul triumphantly victorious over all that men could do to him.

But if Paul wrote out of that background, think also of what he had seen:

He had seen that jailer at Philippi fall on his knees to ask what he must do to be saved. And he had been saved.

He had seen churches established in Europe and Asia.

He had seen a demented girl turned into a rational creature.

He had seen the cynical intellectuals at Athens who laughed at him also yield some people of faith.

He had seen the wicked and corrupt Corinth, known as the prostitute of the world, become the site of a church.

No wonder he was proud of the gospel! He had seen it work.

And that is our affirmation of the gospel. It works.

Martin Luther was an Augustinian monk in Germany. He did everything he could to earn his salvation. But he felt frustrated, unfulfilled, and unsatisfied. So he went on a pilgrimage to Rome.

While at Rome he did everything he could to earn merit. He visited sacred sites; he prayed; he viewed holy relics. One of the things he did was to visit the Scala Sancta, the sacred stairs, supposedly the stairs on which Pilate stood when he sentenced Jesus. As prescribed, he climbed the stairs on his hands and knees, kissing each stair, and repeating prayers as he climbed them.

But all the while a text he had found while preparing lectures on the Book of Galatians kept running through his mind: "The just shall live by faith . . . . The just shall live by faith."

Finally, he stood erect on the stairs and said aloud, "The just shall live by faith . . . . The just shall live by faith," walked down the stairs, and went back to Germany to launch the Protestant Reformation. The gospel worked in his life.

Assurance

Also, when you think of the gospel as dynamite you have an assurance that the gospel is the power of God.

Power was a strange word to use of the gospel when the Roman legions tramped down every road. It would seem that at that time power was with Rome. But where is Rome today? And where is the gospel?

People often search for power.

Is it in military might? Look at the fallen military powers of the world: Carthage, Rome, Nazi Germany, Japan.

Is it in political power? Most observers feel that former President Richard Nixon's fall was due to his obsession with power. Look at Nixon today.

Is it in economic strength? Fortunes have been made and lost. And so have people. Clovis Chappell, the great Methodist preacher, told of a young man who came out of the Ozark Mountains in his early manhood with the firm purpose of making a fortune. Gold became his god, and putting it first, he won it. He came to be worth millions. Then the crash came, and he was reduced to utter poverty. His reason tottered and fell along with his fortune. A mere beggar, he took to the road. One day a policeman found him on Eads Bridge in Saint Louis gazing down into the waters of the Mississippi. He ordered him to move on. "Let me alone," he answered, "I am trying to think. There is something that is better than gold, but I have forgotten what it is." They placed him in an institution for the insane. They knew that a man who could forget *that* was not himself.

In contrast to all of these concepts of power we have the gospel, going its way, exploding into the lives of people, blowing old ways of life, old patterns, old sins into smithereens. It's dynamite!

Activity

Paul affirmed that the gospel was the power of God unto salvation. When you think of the gospel as dynamite, you see activity.

That is the first activity of God's powerful, dynamic gospel: it brings salvation.

One New Year's Eve a son and I joined my other son and my father-in-law in Toledo Bend Lake on the border of Louisiana and Texas for a last gasp duck hunt. We left in shirt sleeves. One son and the father-in-law were already there and had hunted in summer-like weather for several days. But that night the weather changed. And when we got up the next morning it was cold, very cold.

All four of us got in the boat while it was still dark and started off to our hunting places. We had gone four miles probably, down the river channel, alongside an old woods road, when we heard a sound strangely like our motor running out of gas. Horribly enough, that is exactly what it was. We paddled over to an island and decided to start our hunt there. By daylight we had seen few ducks fly and we were extremely cold.

Then the grandfather and the younger boy took the boat and used the trolling motor to return to the camp. To lighten the load one boy and I stayed on the island. Supposedly, we were to shoot ducks as they flew over or landed at the pothole. Actually, we tried to keep warm. Since none of us smoke we had no matches with which to build a fire. We walked a lot to keep the blood circulating and to create a little warmth. We found some trees to shield us a little from the wind. But mostly we just stayed cold.

Four hours later they returned in the boat. We were delivered! After being island castaways in the middle of Toledo Bend Lake for four hours we were saved.

That is what salvation means. It is a deliverance. We were delivered from the island and the cold. When Christ saves us he delivers us from our sin.

We have been in the power of sin, self, and Satan. When Jesus is accepted as Savior, He delivers us from that and gives us salvation.

From the Greek word for power comes *dynamite:* God breaking into our lives.

But there is another activity of God's powerful gospel: giving us strength every day.

Dynamo also comes from the same word for power. A dynamo continually and constantly pumps out power to a life.

Some of us who have known the power of God in salvation have failed to use the power of God in our daily lives. Professing Christ we may also make a shambles of the Christian convictions: drinking, lusting, lying, cheating, manipulating. Why? There are two reasons: you may not really try to change or you have not depended on the power of God to help you change. But God's power is an activity at work daily in your lives.

Acceptance

When you think of the gospel as dynamite you come to an acceptance, too. Paul showed the inclusiveness of the gospel. It was for all people, both Jews and Greeks or Gentiles.

If it is so inclusive, how do you receive it? By believing. Everyone who believes in Jesus Christ, who expresses faith in Him can know this power of God working salvation in his life.

William Wallner grew up in Europe and became a Lutheran minister in Prague, Czechoslovakia. Ken Olsen told a part of his story in *Can You Wait Till Friday?* At first his congregation was small, but not for long. If ever God used a man, He used Dr. Wallner. Hitler was coming to power in Germany and soon Wallner was preaching five sermons on Sunday to over 25,000 people in different languages. In his parish were over 3,000 Jews, including a rabbi, who had become Christians. This was an unusual ministry, caring for refugees who came by the thousands to escape Hitler. One of these was a talented and proud young Jewish man named Karl Loes from Frankfurt. He had been an outstanding drama and art critic, and his word could make or break a beginning star. He told Dr. Wallner he did not want to become a Christian, and was embarrassed to ask for help. However, he did become a Christian and a powerful leader with university students. When Hitler came to Czechoslovakia Karl Loes fled for his life and Wallner lost track of him.

Pastor Wallner stayed as long as he could in Czechoslovakia. He accomplished a heroic action when he discovered that a number of Jewish children were to be taken out in the cold of December and left to freeze to death in a ditch. Quickly, Pastor Wallner arranged through the underground to have the Allies fly them out to safety under the noses of the Nazis. He has been honored by having an olive grove planted in his honor by the state of Israel.

At the end of the war a group of underground fighters were discovered in a cellar and were murdered by the Nazis, who left in disorganized retreat. On the walls were messages written in various languages, and Wallner was asked to translate them. One of the poems stopped him cold, for this is what he read:

> I believe in the sun when it is not shining.
> I believe in love, when I do not feel it.
> I believe in my Lord, Jesus, even when He is silent.

It was signed by Karl Loes. Wallner wept at this last tragic meeting with his long-lost friend, but there was also wonderment at the faith of this man who had soared to such great heights.

It's dynamite! And this power of God can be known in your life if you believe in Christ. Won't you believe today?

PART II
Some Evangelistic Stories

. . .Regarding the Need of Salvation

10
Wages of Sin

Let me tell you about a man who believed that the wages of sin were sweet—Ernest Hemingway, the talented writer. "Papa Hemingway" they called him.

In 1956 a magazine for men described Hemingway somewhat like this: "'What is immoral' says Ernest Hemingway, 'is what you feel bad after.'" By this yardstick, Hemingway was a man of unimpeachable morals. For many years he had hit the bottle, lived with different women, enjoyed such organized carnage as war and bullfighting and had felt pretty good about it all.

"People with different ideas about morality would call him a sinner, and the wages of sin, they say, is death. Hemingway has cheated death time and time again, to become a scarred and bearded legend, a great white hunter, a husband of four wives, a winner of Nobel and Pulitzer prizes. Sin has paid off for Hemingway . . . ."

In June 1966, ten years later, the same magazine reviewed the book, *Papa Hemingway*, by A.E. Hotchner: "In it he described Hemingway's later years: several attempted suicides, the trip to Mayo Clinic, and Ernest babbling around at 70 percent of mental efficiency. In his last few months, he had delusions that the Feds were pursuing him and wiretapping his phone, that his friends were conspiring against him—all these emotional and psychic tragedies caving in on him. The first night back in his Ketchum, Idaho, hideaway he did what he kept telling people he was going to do."

Look closely. See the muscular figure, the salt-and-pepper beard, lying face down in his own blood with his own rifle in his own hand, and his own finger on the trigger. As the magazine said ten years earlier, "Sin has paid off for Hemingway."

He had thought that "forbidden fruits were sweet," but he found in the end that they were bitter. He thought he could laugh at God, but somewhere between the trigger and his brain he found that "the wages of sin is death."

Robert L. Cargill, *All the Parables of Jesus*, (Nashville: Broadman Press, 1970), pp. 27-28.

11
The Necessity of a Commitment

One of my favorite columnists is Ellen Goodman whose three columns a week for the *Boston Globe* have been syndicated nationwide. In one of her recent articles she wrote about a friend who was allergic to making commitments. When his friends chided him about this, he had a rather flip explanation. He said he viewed life as a huge buffet line where a person who made commitments could be compared to the man who filled his plate at the beginning of the line with rather ordinary fare and then after his plate was full came upon all sorts of interesting food which he liked better. With this seemingly irrefutable illustration of his position, the man let people know that all he was really doing was "keeping his options open." Ellen Goodman's evaluation was that another way of describing his action was that he was "coming to the end of the line with an empty plate."

Kenneth Chafin, *How to Know When You've Got It Made* (Waco, Texas: Word Books, 1981), p. 30

12
The Enemy of the Best

A tragic thing happened during a recent Byron Nelson Golf Tournament. A massive tree limb broke off and fell on a number of spectators. Several people were hurt and one man was killed.

It happened near the third hole. Charles Coody was playing the hole at the time of the accident. Shortly after the accident, he was interviewed on the radio. In talking to Frank Glieber, he said, "I heard the limb crack and then fall, and along with a number of spectators we ran over to see what we could do to help." Following the accident, Mr. Coody said, "I had no desire to play after that . . . all of a sudden those three-foot putts didn't seem important." Sportscaster Frank Glieber added his "amen" to the statement of Charles Coody.

It's not always easy for us to appraise what's really important in life. Sometimes it takes a tragedy to make us stop and think.

The real enemy of the best in your life and mine is not the bad, but the good. Many times we allow the trivial to usurp the place of the important. There are times when we allow the trivial to take the place of that which is supremely important in life. This is tragic.

Jesus Christ encourages us to live well-rounded lives, but He cautions us to keep things in their proper perspective. Christ said "Seek ye first the kingdom of God, . . . and all these things shall be added unto you" (Matt. 6:33).

When we get "all these things" out of the proper sequence, they bring little or no real happiness to us in life.

James L. Plietz, "The Enemy of the Best," *Park Cities Baptist Church Journal* (Dallas, Texas, May 15, 1981), p. 1.

13
Suffering from the Wrong Diagnosis

How often is truth stranger than fiction! Such was certainly the case with Dennis Soyster of Laurel, Maryland. Listen to his tale of woe which, obviously, was much too incredible not to be true (from *Saturday Review,* November 10, 1979, p. 8).

Told by the attending physician that he had an incurable disease, Soyster promptly panicked, stole $29,000 from his employer, and proceeded to forget his grief in a riot of pleasure, spending up to $1,000 an evening in one last fling before the end. Hauled into court for embezzlement, Soyster could only plead guilty because, as his lawyer put it, he had "gone off the deep end."

This compulsive binge might have been excusable, or at least understandable, in retrospect had not Soyster turned out to be perfectly healthy. As matters would have it, the only thing he was suffering from was faulty diagnosis. Instead of having some fatal malady, Soyster's problem was that he was allergic to the surgical gloves used in the exploratory operation. Throughout this bizarre episode, he had been reacting to the treatment rather than to the disease!

William E. Hull, "Death Be Not Cheap," *Church Chimes,* First Baptist Church, Shreveport, Louisiana, March 29, 1980, p. 3.

14
His Own Worst Enemy

The Associated Press once carried this brief article:

"Marshall G. Cummings, Jr., has no one but himself to blame for his less-than-successful court appearance.

"Cummings, 25, accused of purse snatching, acted as his own attorney yesterday. As he cross-examined the victim, he asked her: 'Did you get a good look at my face when I took your purse?'

"The Tulsa, Oklahoma jury convicted Cummings and gave him a ten-year prison sentence."

At least he has no one to blame but himself.

We usually find somebody. If something is lost at our house, I'm sure my wife hid it. If there is a new scratch on the car, I'm sure the kids did it. In fact, about the only mistake I can't find somebody else to blame for is cutting myself while shaving.

("By the way, dear, did you forget again to buy me some new blades?")

We're just like that. We don't like to be wrong; and if we are, our anger has to go somewhere, and if it has to go somewhere, we'd like it to get on somebody else, not us.

The story of the crucifixion is really about that. The one who was innocent took the anger of those who were guilty. Sin, our own worst enemy, killed Jesus, our own best friend.

Conversion gets all that straight. We recognize ourselves as guilty and Him as innocent; we accept His suffering for our sins; we begin to learn how to act responsibly as His child.

It's a good thing to know who your own worst enemy is. And your own best Friend.

Clyde E. Fant, "His Own Worst Enemy," *Baptist Standard*, First Baptist Church, Richardson, Texas, edition, March 23, 1977, p. 1.

15
Souls: Weight or Worth

Did you ever wonder how much a soul weighs? Well, thanks to new scientific information this matter can now be settled.

Dr. Nils-Olaf Jacobson, a Swedish doctor from Dusseldorf gives this answer in a book entitled *Life After Death*. He says that a soul weighs twenty-one grams (about three-fourths of an ounce).

This is the way he proved it. He placed the deathbeds of terminal patients on extremely sensitive scales. As they expired, and the soul left their bodies, the scales showed a drop of twenty-one grams.

In an article in the "Significa" column in *Parade* magazine by Irving Wallace and his children David Wallechinsky and Amy Wallace the answer was also given to the question of how much a soul weighs. Citing the experiments of Dr. Duncan MacDougall of Haverhill, Massachusetts, also showed a weight of about three-fourths of an ounce.

Dr. MacDougall performed his experiments with dying tuberculosis patients in a large hospital. He, too, placed the beds on a sensitively balanced platform beam scale then kept close watch on the patient in his final hours. At the precise moment of death the beam fell. With the experiment performed on six patients over two and one-half years the average weight was about three-quarters of an ounce. He even tested his experiments by repeating it on fifteen dogs, which according to traditional Judeo-Christian teachings have no souls. The dogs showed no weight loss at death.

The important question, however, is not the weight of a soul but the worth of a soul.

How much is a soul worth?

Jesus warned us that a soul is worth all of life. He said, "For what shall it profit a man, if he shall gain the whole world, and lose his own soul?" (Mark 8:36). That makes a soul worth a lot.

Once before the Bible tells us about weighing a soul. God startled Belshazzar, king of Babylon, with a bit of handwriting on the wall, letting the proud monarch know that he had been weighed in the balances and found wanting. His soul was worth more than he had reckoned it.

To Jesus a soul was worth giving His life. Jesus gave His life on the cross for the salvation of souls. Any person has value to Him. Any soul is worth His life. That is a pretty high cost for a soul.

A soul. What is the significant thing about it—weight or worth? From the perspective of the Christian faith we would say that a soul's worth is more important than its weight. Believing this, let us be busy about our commission to witness of the Christ who saves souls to these souls of worth.

16
When the Savior Leads
Like a Shepherd

Following the Civil War, Ira Sankey became famous for his gospel singing. In 1875, on a calm, starlit December evening, he was traveling by steamboat up the Delaware River. Many passengers were on the deck. Sankey was asked to sing, and, as always, he consented. As he stood by one of the funnels of the boat, he raised his eyes toward the heavens in quiet prayer. He wanted to sing a Christmas song but, somehow, against his will he was driven to sing the shepherd song, "Savior, Like a Shepherd Lead Us."

After the song had ended, a man with a rough, weather-beaten face came up and asked, "Did you ever serve in the Union Army?"

"Yes," answered Sankey, "in the spring of 1862."

"Can you remember if you were doing picket duty on a bright moonlight night in 1862?"

"Yes," answered Mr. Sankey, very much surprised.

"So was I," said the stranger, "but I was serving in the Confederate Army. When I saw you standing at your post, I thought to myself, *That fellow will never get away from here alive.* I raised my gun and took aim. I was standing in the shadows, while the full bright light of the moon was shining upon you. At that instant, just as a moment ago, you raised your eyes toward heaven and began to sing. I took my finger off the trigger. 'Let him sing his song to the end,' I said to myself, 'I can shoot him afterward. He is my victim and my bullet cannot miss him.' But the song you sang then was the one you sang just now. I heard the words perfectly:

We are thine; do thou befriend us,
 Be the guardian of our way;
Keep thy flock, from sin defend us,
 Seek us when we go astray.

"Those words stirred up many memories in my heart. I thought of my childhood and my God-fearing mother. I had heard her sing that song many times. When you finished your song, it was impossible for me to take aim at you again. I thought: *The Lord who is able to save that man from certain death must surely be great and mighty.* My arm, of its own accord, dropped limp at my side.

"I remembered it all as I heard you sing just now; and your song has wounded my heart. Now I wish that you would help me find a cure for my sick soul."

Deeply moved, Sankey threw his arms about the man, who in the days of the war had been his enemy. That Christmas Eve, the two went vicariously to Bethlehem's manger and on to Calvary's cross. There the stranger found the Savior, the Good Shepherd, who seeks for the lost sheep until He find it. His faith became that proclaimed in the song:

Thou hast promised to receive us,
 Poor and sinful though we be;
Thou hast mercy to relieve us,
 Grace to cleanse, and pow'r to free.

Robert L. Cargill, *Understanding the Book of Hebrews,* (Nashville: Broadman Press, 1967), pp. 83-84.

17
Going Home

Perhaps you are familiar with the story of a French soldier who was found suffering from amnesia. When he was picked up at a railroad station, he looked at his questioners blankly, and all he could say was: "I don't know who I am. I don't know who I am." Because he had been disfigured by facial wounds, there were three different families who claimed him as belonging to them. So he was taken to one village after another where these different families lived, and allowed to walk around by himself. Finally, when he entered the third village, a sudden light of recognition came into his eyes, he walked unerringly down a side street, in through a tidy gate, and up the steps of his father's home. Like the prodigal son, he had "come to himself." The old, familiar surroundings had restored his mind. Once again, he knew who he was and where he belonged.

David E. Roberts, *The Grandeur and Misery of Man* (New York: Oxford University Press, 1955), pp. 20-21.

18
The Cost of Peace with God

Some time ago the First Baptist Church in Shreveport, Louisiana, received the following letter. Enclosed in the letter was a nickel.

"During the last few years the Baptist Tea Room was open, I lived in Shreveport and ate there regularly. The food was delicious. There was one time the lady cashier gave me five cents change too much and I knew it, knowing all the time I was doing wrong. I am sending it to you today so that I can have peace with God about this. Your friend in Christ."

How much does it cost to have peace with God? Apparently for this individual, peace with God cost a nickel.

Over the years what he had done dishonestly had bothered him, weighing heavily on his conscience. With the return of the money the conviction was relieved, his conscience was clear, and he had peace with God.

There are times when it will take more than that to clear a conscience and to ease conviction. But that is a start. And all should make the effort.

What does it cost to have peace with God? It cost Jesus His life. Listen to the Scriptures:

"Now that we have been put right with God through faith, we have peace with God through our Lord Jesus Christ" (Rom. 5:1, GNB).

For peace with God you must accept Christ as Savior who has provided peace by His death on the cross. Peace with God costs a good bit. It cost Christ His life. It costs you commitment of life to Christ.

James E. Carter, *People Parables* (Grand Rapids, Mich.: Baker Book House, 1973), p. 7.

19
Saved at Great Cost

Years ago a mother was carrying her baby over the hills of South Wales, England. She never reached her destination. She was trapped in a blizzard, lost her way, and froze to death. The searchers who found her frozen body marveled that she wore no outer garments to protect her from the cold. When she was lifted, they discovered the reason why. She had taken her coat to wrap her baby and then covered him from the storm with her own body.

The infant was David Lloyd George who became prime minister of Great Britain during World War I. He became one of England's great statesmen and made a vital contribution to humanity. He was always conscious that his life had been spared by the sacrifice of his mother, and that he had been saved for a purpose.

Robert L. Cargill, *Understanding the Book of Hebrews* (Nashville: Broadman Press, 1967), p. 74.

20
Are You Covered?

One January day on my birthday, of all times, I let my foot get a little heavy coming across a bridge leading into downtown Fort Worth. Sitting in a car at the foot of the bridge, a little removed from immediate view, was one of Fort Worth's Finest observing the flow of traffic and monitoring the speed of the cars. I saw him about the time I passed him. Then he announced his presence to me, and unfortunately to others around me, by deciding to drive behind me with all those pretty little lights flashing away.

Standing on the side of the street I produced my driver's license which I fortunately had renewed on time. After listening to his understanding of how fast I went over bridges he then asked for my proof of insurance. Feeling very smug, I reached into the car pocket for it. I knew it was current, too, for I had just paid it a few days earlier. As it turned out, I had paid the premium but I had not put the little slip of paper that serves a proof of insurance in the car pocket. It showed the expiration date of the policy as January 16. That was January 19. He gave me a citation for that.

I paid the fine for the speeding ticket and protested the citation for failure to have proof of insurance coverage. On that issue I requested a hearing before the municipal judge. All of that occurred in January. The trial was set for June.

So one June afternoon I went to Municipal Court 2 to plead my case. When the clerk called my name I went to the desk. She asked me one question: "Did you have valid automobile insurance coverage on January 19?" I replied that I did and proved it by producing the policy statement showing that the new policy was in force from January 16 through July 16. She then said one word, a nice reassuring word: *Dismissed.* And I left the courtroom.

As I walked out of the Municipal Court Building with the reassurance that I was neither charged nor fined for that violation because I was covered by insurance all the time I had another reassuring thought. There will be another time at some distant date in the future when I will stand before another Judge, the Judge of all the universe. There, too, I will hear the word *Justified,* because I am covered by the blood of Jesus Christ, the Son of God who is my Savior. Because He died on the cross for me and because I have accepted Him by faith as my Savior, His blood has covered my violations, in fact, all my sin. On Judgment Day, the Creator of all the universe and the Judge of all humankind will pronounce me and all other believers justified because we are covered by Christ's death.

Listen to the way the apostle Paul expressed it:

> Then as one man's trespass led to condemnation for all men, so one man's act of righteousness leads to acquittal and life for all men. For as by one man's disobedience many were made sinners, so by one man's obedience

many will be made righteous. Law came in, to increase the trespass; but where sin increased, grace abounded all the more, so that, as sin reigned in death, grace also might reign through righteousness to eternal life through Jesus Christ our Lord (Rom. 5:18-21, RSV).

The thought of Judgment is not a frightening idea but a reassurance to the believer. Faith in Jesus Christ has brought justification. The believer is covered by the blood of Jesus Christ. And that gives hope. Are you covered?

21
A Cross for All Nations

In the ancient city of Jerusalem there are two sites that are purported to be Golgotha, the place of the skull, where Jesus was crucified. One of them is in the Church of the Holy Sepulchre, an old, old church building within the walls of the old city. The argument for this site is that the city walls were in a different location in the first century since Jesus was crucified outside the city walls.

The second, and more recently claimed site, is Gordon's Calvary. It is a small hill with a rounded top. Caves in the side of the hill can give the whole hill a skull-shaped appearance when viewed from a little distance. A garden with a tomb carved out of rock known as the Garden Tomb is located next to it. Evangelicals generally opt for this location, while Catholic and Orthodox folks go for the church site.

When you walk through the garden surrounding the Garden Tomb to an observation point from which you get a good view of the skull-shaped hill there is a large sign quoting the crucifixion story from the New Testament. It is written in Greek, Hebrew, and English.

When Jesus was crucified Pilate put a sign on the cross

indicating that the person being executed was "Jesus of Nazareth the King of the Jews" (John 19:19). Customarily the reason for the execution was placarded on the person's cross. The charge brought against Jesus that struck home to Pilate was that He was claiming to be a king. Rome could have no king but Caesar. Insurrection was a serious charge in Rome's eye. This sign was written in three languages: Greek, Hebrew, and Latin.

Interestingly enough, the current sign telling why Jesus died is written in three languages as was the original. But they are not the same three languages. Greek was the universal language of the day when Jesus was crucified. The New Testament was written in Greek. Hebrew was spoken by the people of the area (actually it was Aramaic, a form of Hebrew in Jesus' day) and has been revived in modern Israel. But Latin is no longer the official language. English has fast become the alternate language for people around the world. But the sign was written, both originally and now, in three languages so that almost anyone who happened by could read it.

The cross of Jesus Christ is a cross for all nations. The message is written in the languages of mankind so all people can hear it and receive it.

The need for salvation is universal. All have sinned.

The solution for sin is also universal. Christ died for all.

The message must be made universal. The cross is for all nations. All can receive salvation and new life through faith in Christ. This is the message of the Easter season.

22
The Inheritance

I have come into an inheritance!

Quite unexpectedly I received a letter from a great-uncle with a cover letter and a check from the estate of a great-aunt who had died more than a dozen years before. In fact, she had died so long ago that it took me awhile to realize who she was.

It seems that her house had been sold. She had no children and her husband was already dead. So according to the laws of her state, her estate was divided among her brothers and sisters. She had six brothers and sisters, of which my grandmother was one. However, my grandmother has been dead for twenty-five years so her portion was divided between her ten children. But my father died twelve years ago. So his portion was divided between my mother, my two sisters, and me. By the time all of that dividing was done I had inherited the grand total of $86.33.

But that is not the only inheritance I have. I have a much greater inheritance than that. It is expressed in 1 Peter 1:3-5 in these words:

> Blessed be the God and Father of our Lord Jesus Christ, which according to his abundant mercy hath begotten us again unto a lively hope by the resurrection of Jesus Christ from the dead, To an inheritance incorruptible, and undefiled, and that fadeth not away, reserved in heaven for you, Who are kept by the power of God through faith unto salvation ready to be revealed in the last time.

This inheritance, too, comes about because of someone's death—the death of Jesus Christ upon the cross for my sins.

It is an undivided inheritance. It is not filtered through the hands of grandparents, parents, aunts, or uncles. It comes directly to me through faith in Christ.

And it is an unending inheritance. My check is cashed. My money is spent. My inheritance is in some object in our house. Not so with my spiritual inheritance. It lasts forever.

We are all inheritors of God's grace. This is our greatest inheritance.

23
Tie a Yellow Ribbon

They were all over the place. Everywhere you looked you could see yellow ribbons: in hair, on lapels, around trees (oak and otherwise), in windows, on the columns outside Hulen Mall in Fort Worth, on the girders of Reunion Tower in Dallas.

Why the yellow ribbons? Yellow ribbons became the symbol of hope, support, and acceptance for the fifty-two Americans who were held hostage in Iran for 444 days. After they were released and home in 1981 the yellow ribbons abounded.

The yellow ribbons symbol came from a song about a man on a bus coming home from prison who had sent word to his wife to tie a yellow ribbon around the old oak tree if she loved and accepted him. If the yellow ribbon was there he would stop and they could begin life again together; if the yellow ribbon was not there he would just stay on the bus and forget about them. But the yellow ribbon was there! Many yellow ribbons were there, in fact. A profusion of yellow ribbons assured him of love and acceptance.

The song is based on an old evangelistic story. I expect I have heard that story in revival meetings about as many times as I have heard that song on the radio. And that is a lot.

The yellow ribbon became a symbol of freedom for the former hostages.

Christians already have a symbol for freedom. It is a cross. The apostle Paul asserted, "For freedom Christ has set us free; stand fast therefore, and do not submit again to a yoke of slavery" (Gal. 5:1, RSV). Christ has called us to freedom and has given us freedom. The symbol for our freedom is a cross.

We are freed from servitude to sin. When Christ forgave us of our sin He freed us from that sin. We don't have to carry the burden of the sin nor the load of guilt from that sin. Forgiveness is complete. We are freed from being held in bondage to sin.

We are freed from the limitations of legalism. That was the problem the Galatian Christians faced: returning to a legalistic religion. But Christ frees us from legalism and introduces us to love. We live in love through the love of Christ.

We are freed from the prison of personality. Self often is our biggest problem. But Christ also frees us from ourselves. He comes to live within us and to infuse us with the power of the Holy Spirit in our lives.

We are freed from the dungeon of the devil. Satan was defeated by the death of Christ on the cross and the resurrection of Christ from the dead. While individual skirmishes and personal battles still go on, the outcome has been decided. Christ has overcome. Victory is ours through faith in Jesus Christ.

Tie a yellow ribbon! Use the symbol of freedom and support. But as you do it, remember that the yellow ribbon was really made possible by red blood. When Christ died on the cross He set us free. We live in that freedom. The symbol for that freedom is a cross. "For freedom Christ has set us free" (Gal. 5:1, RSV).

24
Getting Jesus
into and out of Your Heart

One of our church ladies who is a first-grade schoolteacher told me of an interesting incident that occurred as the school year got under way.

The mother of one of her first-grade girls visited her before school began. The mother made the visit to tell the teacher that the girl had open-heart surgery during the summer. Therefore, she would both desire and deserve a little extra care. The mother went on to say that the girl had accepted Christ as Savior and had been baptized shortly before her surgery. Of course she was apprehensive about the surgery but had managed to keep it to herself.

The day before the surgery the surgeon again met with the child and explained exactly what he would do. He would make her heart strong like other boys and girls so she could do the things the other boys and girls did.

The girl seemed a little upset and the doctor inquired about what was bothering her. She said, "I just accepted Christ as my Savior and Jesus now lives in my heart. When you cut open my heart you won't let Jesus out, will you?"

To which the physician replied, "Sweetheart, if Jesus Christ is in your heart, there is no way that anyone else can get Him out of your heart."

And there isn't. The theological term we use for it is the eternal security of the believer. The catch phrase that is used for it which, like all catch phrases, does not adequately express it is "once saved, always saved."

The experience we have had with it is that the nature of the salvation experience is such that whenever you accept Christ as your personal Savior and are born into the kingdom of God you can't be unborn. Once Jesus has come into your heart, someone else can't get Him out of it.

How do you express the salvation experience? It is so comprehensive, all inclusive, and life changing that it is difficult to express. The way the children say it:—that Jesus comes to live in your heart—isn't bad.

How do you express the eternal nature of salvation? That, too, gets difficult to put into words. To say that once

Jesus has come to live in your heart, no one can let Him out isn't bad. After all, your heart does become His home and He lives within you throughout all of life and into eternity.

...Regarding
Repentance in Salvation

25
When You Need to Wash ...
and Repent

My wife's nephew was probably five or six years of age at the time that the family was gathered at a lake for a family holiday celebration on the Fourth of July. Always a big fisherman, this nephew was on the pier or the waterfront when lunchtime came. Called to lunch he reluctantly approached the house. As he reached the front door his aunt said, "Wash your hands. It is time for lunch." To which he replied, "Why? I haven't touched anything dead."

Many of us feel the same way about repentance toward God. Until the time that we have done something gross and dirty and obviously wrong we see little need for repentance. To our way of thinking, repentance is for the person whose hands are fouled by the stench of death; or the canker of theft; or the corruption of lies; or the gangrene of greed. Little do we realize that we, too, need an attitude of repentance toward God.

John the Baptist once called the people to repentance. He challenged them to prove their repentance by changed lives. He reminded them that his baptism was a baptism that signified repentance.

John the Baptist's call teaches us of the continued need for repentance. The persons who need to repent are not just those who have committed heinous crimes or gross sins. The ones who need to repent are all of us. We have met those in need of repentance, and they are us.

Our need for repentance lies at the very roots of our existence. For the ways we have distorted the call of God, for the ways we have digressed from the will of God, for the ways we have disregarded the teachings of God, for the ways we have diminished our witness to God, for the ways we have diluted our mission for God, we need to repent.

Basic to this is the realization that these things have occurred in subtle, soft, almost imperceptible ways. Usually without realizing it we may have shifted away from our focus and our commitment. For most of us these have not been radical swings and dramatic pronouncements, but subtle shifts and unacknowledged distances from our center. That calls for repentance, confession, and new commitment.

Don't wait until you have touched something dead before you wash your hands for lunch. Good hygiene demands that. And don't wait until you have committed a horrible sin to repent. Good spiritual health demands that.

26
When God Answers the Parentheses Rather than the Prayer

One of the greatest stories in Christian literature is the story of Augustine. He was a lively young man, debonair and sophisticated. And like all the upper-crust young men of his century and generation, he had a mistress. His first mistress he kept for sixteen years. And after he got tired of her he got another and later, as I recall it, yet another. Now Augustine also liked to go to church on Sunday and hear Bishop Ambrose preach. Ambrose had the ability to lift a man out of himself to the point of thinking, "I want that"; and to make him reach for spiritual things. So Augustine got into a conflict with himself. He would pray, "O Lord, I want Thee. I will give myself to Thee." But in his mind there was a little parentheses: he was not going to give up his mistress. So God answered not the prayer, but the parentheses. He didn't give Augustine spiritual power.

But Augustine, a great soul, finally fought the battle through. One day he got down on his knees and prayed and gave the Lord his whole self including that parentheses. And the minute he did that, the faucet was connected and the power flowed.

So everyone must choose. If you give God the parentheses you will "walk in newness of life."

Norman Vincent Peale, "God Can Reactivate Your Life" (New York: Foundation for Christian Living), 1963, p. 9.

27
Pardon Must Be Received

In 1829 two men—Wilson and Porter—were convicted of robbing the United States mails, and sentenced to death by hanging. Three weeks before the time set for Wilson's execution, he was pardoned by President Andrew Jackson. Wilson refused the pardon.

His case was brought before the Supreme Court. The court handed down this decision: "A pardon is a deed, to the validity of which delivery is essential, and delivery is not complete without acceptance. It may be rejected by the person to whom it is tendered; and if it is rejected we have discovered no power in this court to force it upon him."

Most folks would agree that George Wilson was foolish for refusing to accept a pardon. Yet every day people reject the pardon which God has provided.

Joe L. Ingram, "Viewpoints," *Baptist Message* (March 11, 1976), p. 9

28
Providing the Terrain for Sin

Claude Bernard, a renowned nineteenth-century French physiologist, believed that disease is resisted by a central equilibrium within the patient. Bernard said, "Illnesses hover constantly about us—they are seeds blown by the wind, but they do not take root in the terrain unless it is ready to receive them." By the terrain, Bernard meant the body, a collection of cells and systems constantly shifting, altering, and adjusting to the pressures from within and without.

Although Louis Pasteur disagreed with Claude Bernard during his lifetime, Pasteur's dying words were these: "Bernard was right. The microbe is nothing, the terrain is everything."

Ken Olson, *Can You Wait Till Friday?* (Greenwich, Conn.: Fawcett Publications, Inc., 1975), p 250.

29
Seeing Yourself as You Are

An anecdote of the war provided a preacher with the picture he wanted in order to show that we see ourselves only when we see ourselves in Christ.

"During the war a soldier picked up on the battlefields of France a battered frame which had once contained a picture of Jesus. The picture was gone but the frame still bore the words *Ecce Homo.* The soldier sent it home as a souvenir, and someone at home put a mirror in it, and hung it on the wall. One day a man went into that house and understood the startling words, *Behold the man,* and saw *himself.* We see ourselves only when we see ourselves in Jesus. Blots we barely knew were there come to view in His white light."

William E. Sangster, *The Craft of Sermon Illustration* (Grand Rapids, Mich.: Baker Book House, reprinted 1973), p 45.

30
Breaking Faith: the Need to Repent

Theodore H. White closed his study of President Richard M. Nixon and the Watergate crisis with these words: "The true crime of Richard M. Nixon was simple: he destroyed the myth that binds America together, and for this he was driven from power.

"The myth he broke was critical—that somewhere in American life there is at least one man who stands for law, the President. That faith surmounts all daily cynicism, all evidence or suspicion of wrongdoing by lesser leaders, all corruptions, all vulgarities, all the ugly compromises of daily striving and ambition. That faith holds that all people are equal before the law and protected by it; and that no matter how the faith may be betrayed elsewhere, at one particular point—the President—justice will be done beyond prejudice, beyond rancor, beyond the possibility of a fix. It was that faith that Richard Nixon broke, betraying those who voted for him even more than those who voted against him."

Theodore H. White, *Breach of Faith* (New York: Atheneum Publications, 1975), p 322.

31
Putting Your Weight on God

My Grandfather Carter lacked but one week being ninety-eight years old at the time of his death.

He was past eighty when he took his first airplane ride. He had been visiting one of his daughters who lived in Kansas City, Missouri, and flew from there to Indianapolis, Indiana, to visit another daughter.

On my next visit to him he told me about the trip. "Son," he said, "I don't put my full weight down on that seat the whole trip."

That is not faith.

Faith is putting your full weight on God. Faith is trusting God without any holding back, without any restraint, without any reservations.

Many of us practice faith the same way my grandfather rode the airplane. We don't really put our full weight down.

For instance, we may give God our problems through prayer—and still worry about them.

We may turn a situation over to God—and still try to second guess the outcome.

We may accept a promise of God—and still try to bring about the result ourselves.

We may say that we accept Christ by faith for salvation —and still try to work our way to heaven.

That is not faith. Faith is belief; it is trust; it is commitment. Faith is giving ourselves completely to God; putting our full weight on Him.

32
A Faith to the End

One of the most thrilling and familiar stories of martyrdom, the martyrdom of Polycarp, bishop of Smyrna, illustrates this truth. In the middle of the second century, during the annual festival of Caesar in Smyrna, Polycarp was seized by the Roman authorities. Even some of the officials tried to persuade Polycarp to recant and to say, "Caesar is Lord." But the old man staunchly refused. When he had entered the arena, the proconsul told him, "Swear, and I will release thee; blaspheme Christ." To this Polycarp replied, "Eighty-and-six years have I served Christ, and He has never done me wrong. How can I blaspheme my King, who saved me?"

After passing judgment on Polycarp, they were about to nail him to the stake to burn him. He said to them, "Leave me as I am, for he that hath granted me to endure the fire will grant me also to endure the pile unmoved, even without the security that ye seek from the nails." So they did not nail him, but tied him to the stake. Then Polycarp offered his last prayer: "O Lord God Almighty, the Father of Thy well-beloved and ever-blessed Son, Jesus Christ, by whom we have received the knowledge of Thee, . . . I thank Thee that Thou hast graciously thought me worthy of this day and of this hour, that I may receive a portion among the number of martyrs, in the cup of Thy Christ."[1]

Note

1. Herbert B. Workman, *Persecution in the Early Church* (New York and Nashville: Abingdon Press, 1960. Apex Books edition), pp. 134-36.

33
The Title Deed of Salvation

The classic biblical definition of faith is found in Hebrews 11:1; "Now faith is the substance of things hoped for, the evidence of things not seen." The Greek word translated "substance" had a technical meaning in the business world of the first century. It referred to one's property or effects. This is seen in the story of the woman named Dionysia told by Kenneth Wuest in *Bypaths in the Greek New Testament.* She was described as a woman of set jaw and grim determination.

Apparently she had lost a case in a local court over a piece of land to which she laid claim. Not satisfied with the decision of a lower court, she determined to take her case to a higher court in Alexandria. She sent her slave to that city, with the legal documents safely encased in a stone box. On the way, the slave lost his life in a fire which destroyed the inn where he had put up for the night. For 2,000 years the sands of the desert covered the ruins of the inn, the charred bones of the slave, and the stone box. Archaeologists uncovered these remains. In the box they found the legal documents. They read the note which this woman had sent to the judge in Alexandria, "In order that my lord the judge may know that my appeal is just, I attach my *hypostasis.*" That which was attached to this note, she designated by the Greek word translated "substance" in Hebrews 11:1. The attached document was translated and found to be the title deed to the piece of land which she claimed as her own possession, the evidence of her ownership.

This is faith: our title deed to salvation in Christ and the mercies and grace of God. The thing for which we earnestly hope is salvation. Faith is the title deed to that great hope, that great reality—the salvation of our own souls.

Wuest, *Bypaths in the Greek New Testament*, pp. 18-19.

34
He Came unto His Own and His Own Received Him Not

Some of the personnel in the athletic offices at Texas Christian University are rather new in Fort Worth and TCU. Being new they may not always be acquainted with some past TCU athletic figures.

One day recently an older gentleman dressed in some of his older, rather rumpled clothes came into one of the offices in the Daniel-Meyer Coliseum at TCU with an armload of newspapers. He dumped the newspapers on the floor, mentioned something about "here are your papers," and moved toward the door when the secretary stopped him. When she questioned him he said that he had read in the newspaper that they were collecting newspapers and that there they were. The secretary then suggested that he pick up the papers; he couldn't leave them there. He didn't take too kindly to that suggestion. The idea of picking the papers up and carrying them to his car then home again did not seem to appeal to him.

Upon hearing the voice in the outer office the younger TCU athletic figure came out to see the cause of disturbance. When the secretary caught him up on the situation then he, too, suggested that the man pick up the papers. He refused to do that. So he was told that he could leave the office. He refused to do that, too.

Whereupon the younger man went to the telephone and called campus security requesting that this man be removed from the office. When the campus security officer arrived he spoke to the older man then said to the younger man that he would get the man out of the office if he really wanted him out, but he would rather not since the older man was Dutch Meyer.

Dutch Meyer was the longtime, legendary, revered former TCU basketball coach. The Daniel-Meyer Coliseum in which they were then standing was named for him. Dutch Meyer was about to be thrown out of his own facility.

There is a verse in the Gospel of John that refers to the coming of Christ into His own world and to His own people. It says: "He came to his own home, and his own people received him not" (John 1:11, RSV).

Let's not be guilty of throwing Christ out of His own place.

35
Accepting Forgiveness

A. Leonard Griffith, in *Beneath the Cross of Jesus*, told of a time when an archbishop of Paris was preaching to a great congregation in Notre Dame. He told the story of three young carefree, worldly, and godless men who wandered into the cathedral one day. Two of the men wagered the third that he would not make a bogus confession. He accepted the wager. The priest, who listened, realized what was happening, so when the pretending penitent had finished, he said, "To every confession there is penance. You see the great Crucifix over there? Go to it, kneel down, and repeat three times as you look up into the face of the Crucified. 'All this you did for me, and I don't care a damn!' "

The young man emerged from the confessional box to report what had happened and to claim the wager from his companions. "Oh no," they said, "first complete the penance, and then we will pay the wager."

Walking slowly to the great crucifix, the young man knelt down and looked up into that face with its searching eyes of aggrieved love. Then he began, "All this you did for me, and I . . ." He got no further. Tears flooded his eyes. His heart was torn by the pain of repentance. There his old life ended, and there the new began.

Finishing his sermon, the archbishop said, "I was that young man.' "

128

Note

Leonard Griffith, *Beneath the Cross of Jesus* (New York and Nashville: Abingdon Press, 1961), pp. 30-31.

36
Forgiveness: Human and Divine

Not long ago a father brought his son into the pastor's office to talk about becoming a Christian. (This is most commendable and it would be well if more fathers took such an interest in the spiritual welfare of their children.)

In the course of the discussion, the pastor sought to establish the relationship between repentance and forgiveness. He thought he would make the point by referring to an incident that could happen in the boy's own life.

"What would happen," asked the pastor, "if you broke a plate of your mother's china, and then you told her that you were really and truly sorry that you had done it?" The boy's answer was as quick as a flash: "She would say, 'That doesn't make a bit of difference; the plate is still broken!'"

Art Linkletter has made a fortune from recording the wise and cute sayings of children. This child's answer was more than cute. It helped to point up the difference between human forgiveness and divine forgiveness.

Often we humans think more of the act that has been performed. Even being sorry afterwards doesn't really make too much difference to us. The deed is committed and the harm is done. But God looks at the heart. When we are truly sorry (repentant), He forgives us and restores us to a right relationship with Himself. That's the difference between human forgiveness and God's forgiveness. But then, that's the difference between people and God.

James E. Carter, *People Parables*, (Grand Rapids: Baker Book House, 1973,) p. 1.

37
"Be Ye Reconciled"

Porter Routh told a touching story about Henry Schnider, a German pastor.

Routh visited East Germany on his way to the Baptist World Alliance in Stockholm. The general secretary of East German Baptists took him to view the infamous Buchenwald concentration camp. This was the place where Hitler's cohorts tried out all their scientific experiments. This was where they saw how individuals would react under all kinds of terrible drugs, and where they experimented about how long persons could go without food or liquids—until they died of starvation or thirst. Here is where they tested how much pain a person could stand when they were operated on without any anesthetics whatsoever. It was here that more than 47,000 people were put to death.

They took Routh to a four by seven-foot cell. On one wall was a picture of Henry Schnider. On the opposite wall was a Scripture verse written in German. The verse read: "Now then we are ambassadors for Christ, as though God did beseech you by us: we pray you in Christ's stead, be ye reconciled to God." Routh was told that at every opportunity Henry Schnider could get a group of prisoners around him, he would talk to them about being reconciled to God through Jesus Christ. And one night they took Henry Schnider out and shot him to death. But the message of Schnider lives on in East Germany—"be ye reconciled to God."

R. Earl Allen, *Messenger* of Rosen Heights Baptist Church, Fort Worth, Texas, September 9, 1977, p. 1.

38
Forgiving Enemies

During one of the persecutions of the Armenians by the Turks, an Armenian girl and her brother were closely pursued by a Turkish soldier. Trapped at the end of a lane, the soldier killed the brother before his sister's eyes. The sister escaped by leaping over a wall and fleeing into the country. She later became a nurse.

One day a wounded Turkish soldier was brought into the hospital where the young woman worked. She recognized him as the soldier who had killed her brother and had tried to kill her. The soldier's condition was such that the least neglect on the part of the nurse would have cost him his life. But she gave him painstaking and constant care.

As he recovered, the soldier recognized her as the girl whose brother he had killed. He asked her why she had taken such good care of him. He had killed her brother. She said she had a religion that taught her to forgive her enemies.

James E. Carter, *Christ and the Crowds* (Nashville: Broadman Press, 1981), pp. 109-110.

39
God's Continual Search

There was a Methodist circuit rider in the South many years ago. He had two boys, and as he used to say, one was always good and one was almost always bad. The bad boy would run away to the nearest circus when his father was gone. The father would find him and without any scolding would simply say, "Ed, come home." This went on intermittently for several years. Then one day when the preacher came home Ed was gone and the only circus was two states away. So the father got on a train and rode for a day and a night to the circus town. Sure enough, there was Ed. "Come home, son," said his father. "Dad," demanded the boy, "how did you find me way out here?" "Why, Ed," said his father, "God always tells me where you are. I will always find you." That broke the boy's stubborn willfulness. "You win," he said. So he went home, attended school, and prepared himself for the ministry. Today he is one of the South's respected preachers.

Gerald Kennedy, *The Parables* (New York: Harper and Row, 1960), pp. 7-8.

40
Finding Forgiveness and Sanity

In the fourth century, Diocletian carried out one of the most severe persecutions of the early Christians by the Roman state. Diocletian's son-in-law, Galerius, urged him to begin the persecutions and insisted that they be continued. Succeeding Diocletian as emperor of Rome, Galerius continued the persecutions with unabated zeal. Galerius had his home in Nicomedia. A young Roman army officer, who was a part of the court of Galerius, was impressed by the faith of the Christians in Nicomedia. He asked them the secret of their courage in face of persecution and death. He was told and received instruction in the Christian faith. When the Christians were next examined, he stepped forward and requested Galerius make a note of his name among the Christians.

"Are you mad?" asked Galerius. "Do you wish to throw away your life?"

"I am not mad," the officer replied. "I was mad once, but am now in my right mind." This young Roman army officer was won to faith in Christ by his observation of the death of the Christians.

Herbert B. Workman, *Persecution in the Early Church* (New York and Nashville: The Abingdon Press, 1960, paperback ed.), pp. 25-26.

41
Claiming Your Inheritance

My wife and I were on vacation in Eastern Tennessee in the Smoky Mountains. We had gone to a restaurant called the Blackberry. We liked it there. One side of the building was all glass and you could look out on the mountains in the evening and have your dinner—just beautiful! The waitress brought the menu and we were looking over this huge menu crawling through the French, trying to find the hamburgers. An old man who looked to be in his eighties, with a shock of white hair, came up to the table.

"Good evening."

Must be the proprieter, I thought. "Good evening."

"You on vacation?"

"Yes"

"Enjoying yourself?"

"Yes."

"Where are you from?"

Well, now that's none of his business, but be polite. "Oklahoma."

"Oklahoma, I've never been to Oklahoma."

I'm thinking, *Well let's keep it that way. I mean we're on vacation, right? Vacation—he's an intruder.*

"What do you do?"

"Well, I teach in the seminary."

"Oh, you teach preachers. I've got a story about a preacher," he said and pulled out a chair.

(You know—"Sure sit at our table while you tell it." Everybody has a story about a preacher, but most of them came out of Noah's Ark on crutches. You wait until they're over, grin, and go on.)

He said, "I was born back here in these mountains. My mother was not married, and the reproach that fell upon her fell upon me. The children at school had a name for me and it hurt; it hurt very much. And during recess I would go and hide in the weeds until the bell rang. At lunchtime I took my lunch and went behind a tree to avoid them.

"When I went to town with my mother, when the women and men would stare at her and then stare at me and they would look at me, I knew they were trying to guess whose child I was.

"Painful time, about seventh or eighth grade. I guess I was in the seventh or eighth grade. I started going to hear a preacher. He frightened me in a way. He attracted me in a way. He wore a claw hammer tailcoat, striped trousers, and had a face that looked like it had been quarried out of the mountain. He thundered.

"I was afraid people would say, 'What's a boy like you doing in church?' So I just went in time for the sermon and then I would rush out.

"One Sunday however, some women had queued up in the aisle and I couldn't get out; and I began to sweat; I began to get cold and sweat; I thought, *Oh somebody is going to say to me, 'What's a boy like you doing in church?'*

"I felt a hand on my shoulder. I looked out of the corner of my eye and saw that beard and saw that face (oh, boy!). That minister stared at me; looked at me; stared at me; and I thought, *Oh no!*

"He said, 'Well boy, you're child of . . . a child of. . . .' Oh wait!' the man said. 'You're a child of God. I see a striking resemblance,' he said. He swatted me on the bottom and said, 'Go claim your inheritance, boy!' "

I said, "Now what's your name?" He said, "Ben Hooper."

Ben Hooper. Ben Hooper. My father had told me about the time when, for two terms, the people of Tennessee had elected an illegitimate governor named Ben Hooper.

Fred B. Craddock, "A Modest Proposal: A Listener Overhears," (v. 3, tape recording, Lyman Beecher Lectures on Preaching, Yale University, 1978. Used by permission of Fred B. Craddock.)

. . .Regarding the Results of Salvation

42
Be Worth Saving

The late Bishop Bruce Baxter once told the story of a small boy whom a stranger rescued from drowning. After artificial respiration had brought the lad back to consciousness, he looked into the face of the man who had saved him from a watery grave, and said, "Thank you, sir, for saving my life!" To which the man replied, "That's all right, son, glad to do it. But see to it that you're worth saving!" With that the stranger walked away.

The boy never forgot those words. For the rest of his life the admonition of the stranger rang in his mind and heart. "That's all right, son, glad to do it. But see to it that you're worth saving!" That boy was Bishop Baxter himself.

Surely every Christian could say, "Thank you, Lord, for saving my soul!" And He replies, "That's all right, my child, glad to do it. But see to it that you are worth saving!" Complete salvation involves not only the saving of the soul but the saving of the life as well. It should be the ambition and joy of every Christian to live every day in such a way that he shows God and the world that he is worth saving.

H. H. Hobbs, "Are You Worth Saving?" (*The Beam*, February, 1961), p. 24.

43
God Changes People

Several years ago a man, who has since become a dear friend, came to the end of his rope. He was in his thirties, he had been an active churchman for years, was very successful in his business life, had a wife and four children, and was contemplating suicide. This man, whom I shall call Jack, was driven to succeed at everything he did, but he hated the person he had become. At this point he met some people with whom he could identify deeply, except they acted as if their lives were just beginning, instead of ending. As a result of being with these people, Jack's life received a second touch.

He decided that he would try to give his future to God, a day at a time. His wife made the same decision, and they prayed together about their lives. Jack just couldn't believe that God could really change a world as fouled-up as he felt his was. And he said so. But he began on faith to learn to live with Christ as the Lord of his life. First, Jack tried to reach out to his family. When he started communicating as a person with his wife, she told him that he had been such a bear with the little ones that for years she had gotten them out of the front of the house when he came home from work. So Jack began to get to know his children.

About two weeks later his twelve-year-old son came in to talk to him. This boy had no friends at school and had begun to steal things from around the neighborhood to get attention. He was almost totally alone. "Dad," he said hesitantly, "what's happened to you lately?" His dad (who had been a tough professional athlete) looked up from his desk. "Well, son," he struggled for the right words, "I—

guess I was making a pretty big mess out of my life and I decided I'd ask God to take it over and show me how to live it."

The boy looked at him and then down at the floor. "Dad," he said quietly, "I think I'd like to do that, too."

The father just stood there with tears running down his cheeks, and he and the boy held each other and wept together. The next day Jack had to go to New York on a business trip for two weeks. On the way back he was anxious to get home. When his plane got in, his son broke through the crowd and ran out on the ramp to meet his father. His eyes were shining with excitement! Hugging him, he said breathlessly, in a kind of grateful wonder, "Daddy, do you know what God has done?"

"No, what son?" his dad asked.

"He's changed every kid in my class!!"

Jack could not wait to tell me this story. "I guess God can change the world," he said smiling.

And I believe He can.

Keith Miller, *A Second Touch* (Waco: Word Books, 1967), pp. 155-156.

────────────

44
What Jesus Does for You Now

I had the question best put to me by a stewardess on a flight from Washington to Los Angeles. The equipment had been changed to a smaller plane than had been scheduled so all the stewardesses were not needed. Those who were not working the flight "dead-headed" back to Los Angeles as passengers. One of them sat by me. She was reading a book on transactional analysis and I was working my way through *Future Shock*. We began to visit.

She was a modern girl in every way. Though she was from a solid family she had decided that marriage was passé. She and her boyfriend had an apartment together, but neither of them was ready for marriage. He felt that there wasn't anything after death, but she wasn't so sure. When I told her that I was a minister she had two questions. First, she wanted to know why I had decided to be a minister. I told her as simply as I could of the experience I had as an eighteen-year-old who was crippled with arthritis and thought the end of my world had come. And then I discovered that God had a wonderful plan for my life.

She listened with interest and then hit me with the big question. "Now tell me as simply as you can, what it is that Jesus Christ does for you right now?" This is not the question that we are often asked, but it is the question which is on the minds of the people we are around. You see, they feel that if Christ can help you in the "nowness" of your life, then maybe He can help them.

I know you're curious about how I answered the girl's question. We talked for an hour, but let me share with you a brief statement of the main points. I must confess that putting into words what Jesus Christ means to me to tell a person who did not have a church background was a challenge. It made me put together in one conversation many things which ordinarily would have been kept separate.

I told her: "There are several things which Jesus Christ does for me right now. First, He helps me accept the fact that I am not perfect. I make mistakes. He forgives my sins day by day as I confess them to Him. Second, He helps me to accept the gifts I have and to use them in a way that gives me a sense of fulfillment. Third, He helps me to love people that I would not have loved before. Fourth, He gives me good friends in the church who love me and care for me in all the circumstances of life. Fifth, He gives meaning to my life beyond my self. Finally, He helps me to accept the fact that I am mortal and will someday die.

He gives me the hope of everlasting life through His resurrection."

Looking back on the conversation there are many things I left out. I should have mentioned the difference Christ makes in my home and other things. I have a feeling that you will not have much trouble thinking in very concrete terms about the difference Christ makes in your life day by day. This ought to be part of your witness.

Chafin, Kenneth L., *The Reluctant Witness* (Broadman Press: Nashville, 1974), pp 41-43.

45
Remember the Cost of Salvation

A story came out of the violence and sadism of a Nazi concentration camp that illustrates the giving of self.

On February 17, 1941, Maximilian Kolbe, the press apostle of Poland, was imprisoned by the gestapo and was taken to Auschwitz. It was noted during the roll call at the end of July that a prisoner had escaped. When one escaped, it was the rule that ten innocent people must die. Without consideration, ten were selected to die in a most cruel way, the death of starvation. One cried out, "Have mercy! I have a wife and children."

Kolbe stepped forward and offered himself to replace this head of a family and to go with the other nine into the hunger bunker. He became their comforter and preacher, their leader and example. He endured the terrible sufferings from hunger and exhaustion in full consciousness for two weeks; then they gave him a deadly injection. He died on August 14.

The hardened Nazi guards noted dully that prisoner 16670 was dead. But the man for whom he sacrificed himself spends each August 14 in reflection and unspeakable gratitude for the one who died for him.

We Christians gratefully remember and serve Him who "offered up himself" (Heb. 7:27) for our sins. Jesus was the perfect priest, and He gave himself as the perfect sacrifice.

Robert L. Cargill, *Understanding the Book of Hebrews* (Nashville: Broadman Press, 1967), pp. 78-79.

46
Growth: The Expected Result of the Christian

I had a great uncle who was a medical doctor in a small town in Arkansas. My grandmother's brother, he was known affectionately as "Uncle" by all nieces and nephews as well as the great-nieces and nephews. He owned the old family home place—the Martin Place—where we lived when I was born. My father was manager of the farm. And "Uncle" delivered me at birth.

"Uncle's" office was on the second floor above the department store run by two of his brothers. To reach the office you climbed a flight of stairs. From the waiting room you went into his private office which was filled with impressive-looking medical books in glass-covered cases. We usually found him seated at his rolltop desk.

As a little boy everytime we visited him in his office, he would listen to my heartbeat then weigh me. If I had gained any weight since the last visit he would give me fifty cents. It took me quite awhile to realize that "Uncle" never kept a record of my weight from visit to visit. Besides, you would expect a healthy, normal, growing boy to weigh more each time you saw him on visits that got increasingly infrequent.

If you expect a child to grow wouldn't you also expect

a child of God to grow? Certainly. That is the expected outcome of the Christian's life. The Christian is expected to grow.

Paul expressed it when he wrote, "We are to grow up in every way into him who is the head, into Christ" (Eph. 4:15, RSV). And Peter had reference to the same thing when he admonished us to "grow in grace and knowledge of our Lord and Savior Jesus Christ" (2 Pet. 3:18, RSV).

If a child does not grow we immediately suspect that something is wrong and get medical diagnosis and treatment.

But what if the Christian does not grow? What if he remains immature in his outlook, unredeemed in his attitude, and undeveloped in the Christian qualities and virtues of life? Unfortunately, too often we excuse that as just the expected rather than the unexpected.

Growth is the expected result for the Christian. Christians should always be making some progress in growth toward the goal of Christlikeness. If you are not, then perhaps some checking up of spiritual health needs to be done.

47
Living Two Lives

Russell Conwell was a Union Army captain during the Civil War. One day he was leading his company in sudden retreat across a burning bridge when he found that he had left his sword behind. A young lad from Vermont dashed through the flames and came back with it; but he died a few days later of his burns. Not long after, Russell Conwell himself lay wounded all night on the field of battle; and faced there the best he had ever seen: a lad, all aflame, sword in hand, legs and arms and face blackened by the fire. And a silent vow went up that if he were spared, he would live his own life and the life of that tall young recruit. After the war he became a newspaper correspondent, a lecturer, a lawyer, now this, now that: but the vision would not fade. It seemed to him that in this queer world there was just one way to live two lives. And so he built a great church in Philadelphia, and a great university. Only at the foot of a cross could he live his own life, and the life of Johnny Ring!

Interpreter's Bible, George A. Buttrick, ed. (New York and Nashville: Abingdon Press, 1952), vol. 8, p. 423

48
God Calls to Life

The summer after I graduated from high school I worked as a feed salesman. One of my customers was the Caddo Parish Penal Farm near Shreveport, Louisiana. Running a little later than usual one day, I arrived there shortly before lunch. After taking the order the superintendent asked if I would stay and eat lunch with them. Acting coy, I mumbled something about having a lunch in the car. Really, I expected him to insist that I stay. But he did not press the invitation.

That evening at supper I told my family about the invitation to eat at the penal farm. My father told me that I had really erred. He told me that they ate well at the penal farm, especially the officers. After that I often made it a point to arrive at the penal farm near the lunch hour, but the invitation was never issued again.

God offers us an invitation to life. When that invitation is accepted life in its fullest and most meaningful sense begins. God's mercy and grace are experienced.

But you have to accept the invitation. Unlike the penal

farm superintendent, God continues to extend the invitation to us. Now we may act coy and try to get God to give us a special invitation with extra insistence. And to tell the truth, He does. In many ways God continues to seek us and ask us to come to Him.

This is God's invitation to life. To accept the invitation is to accept life, to open the way to life-giving and life-enriching experiences. To reject the invitation is to close the door to life. Some things are self-inviting by their very nature. Accept God's invitation. Open the door to life.

49
God's Peace Stands Guard

Ralph A. Herring was the son of missionary parents who served in China. Even though he did not identify the small boy, I suspect he was giving a personal testimony in this comment on Philippians 4:7.

During the revolution of China in 1911, a small boy was fleeing with his missionary parents from the interior to safety in Shanghai. For months the troops of the north passed through the city where he had lived on their way to the front. Alarming rumors of bloodshed and disorder had filled his heart with anxiety. The train on which his parents and a few other missionaries were riding had special permission to pass through the lines en route to Hankow. He saw the opposing armies drawn up in battle array, and the bullet scars on the buildings when he arrived in Hankow. That night the city was quiet. The fighting had passed farther north, and a contingent of British soldiers, supported by a warship standing by on the Yangtze River, had things in hand. Outside his window the measured tread of a British guard assured him that he and his loved ones could rest in perfect safety, and all fear was gone as he lay down to sleep.

God is like that. He sets a garrison of peace to stand guard over our hearts and our thoughts in Christ Jesus.

Ralph A. Herring, *Studies in Philippians* (Nashville: Broadman Press, 1952), pp. 99-100.

. . .Regarding the Witness to Salvation

50
The Value of an Incidental Witness

"Testimony" was an English preacher's theme when he made use of the following personal illustration that shows we are not always aware how far our witness may reach, and words that seem lost on the air often have astonishing usefulness. He said:

"I was preaching in Plymouth some time ago. I lived in Leeds at the time. Wandering a little disconsolately around a city in which I have few friends, I decided to slip into a telephone call box and have three minutes' conversation with my wife. It is a long way from Plymouth to Leeds and as I waited for the operator to thread the call through the various exchanges of the Midlands—supposing the line to be sealed—I murmured verses of favorite hymns to myself to while the time away.

'My knowledge of that life is small,
    The eye of faith is dim;
But 'tis enough that Christ knows all,
    And I shall be with Him.'

Suddenly, from somewhere in the Midlands a voice vibrant with unspeakable sadness startled me broad awake by calling out over the line: 'Say it again. Say it again.'

"I held the instrument more firmly and said with immense earnestness:

'My knowledge of that life . . .'

As I finished the verse, the same piteous voice called back: 'Thank you! Thank you!'

"Cast on the air . . . and picked up! Uttered in all unconsciousness that it could be overheard, and it became a blessing. It is a picture of how God employs our witness. He contrives His own use of what we do. Many an obscure disciple has lived a life of winsome loveliness all unaware that he was watched, heard, appreciated . . . ."

William E. Sangster, *The Craft of Sermon Illustration* (Grand Rapids, Mich.: Baker Book House, 1973), pp. 42-43.

51
The Call that Is Never Finished, Never Silent

You stand in the Market Square of medieval Krakow, Poland, in the shadow of the Gothic-style Cloth Hall. Atop the 250-foot tower of St. Mary's Church, a lone man sounds his trumpet four times to the four corners of the city.

Just so, in the year 1241 a trumpeter warning the city of approaching Tartar invaders was suddenly interrupted in his call—slain by an enemy arrow. The unfinished fanfare still marks every hour today in Krakow in memory of that hero. It has echoed across the ancient rooftops for more than seven centuries.

It is the trumpet call to arms, never finished, yet never silenced in 700 years.

So the call of Jesus and of Paul was interrupted, the call to go into all the earth and make disciples of all nations. This, too, is the trumpet call to arms—never finished, yet never silenced.

Clyde Fant, "Thinking Together" (*The Baptist Standard*, FBC, Richardson, Texas Ed., November 30, 1977), p. 1.

52
Getting the Message of Life Across

The little girl who isn't crazy about a birthday party is yet to be born.

So the Garcias of Chicago made elaborate, maybe even a little garish, plans for their daughter's fifth birthday. From a slim salary, trappings appropriate to such occasions—balloons, noisemakers, refreshments, etc.—were bought and held in readiness for the grand day. A gift—probably modest, inexpensive, and much-wished-for—was wrapped and tucked away in some safe place, out of the reach of grubby hands and beyond the gaze of prying eyes. Neighborhood kids were invited and sternly warned to keep their mouths shut about the big event. Mama and Daddy Garcia wanted the extravaganza to be a surprise; they could just see those tiny black eyes pop out on stems when the kids began to gather and it dawned on their queen-for-a-day that this, all of it, was for her.

But things didn't work out as planned.

The Garcias live—or lived—on the third floor of one of those terrible high-rise apartment complexes where there are no yards, no porches, no balconys—just miles of corridors and endless rows of windows and doors and dark brick and drab. Because the honoree was wild about broiled hamburgers, her father tried to humor her by preparing her favorite dish. But he made the terrible mistake of lighting an outdoor grill inside the apartment. The result was catastrophic. An explosion ripped through a nearby wall and turned the building into a towering inferno.

The fire department's rescue squad did its best to avert

the tragedy, or at least to minimize it. But by then there wasn't much that could be done.

When it was all over and officials worked at the grim job of making identifications, someone noticed that a fire escape, a perfectly good one, was fastened to the wall right outside the Garcias' window. It had gone unused. They did not know it was there.

Why didn't their neighbors shout to them and tell them that safety was within arm's reach? They did. But they screamed in English. The Garcias understood nothing but Spanish. The message that could have meant life never got through.

The same tragic thing can happen and does happen to the saving Word. It is possible for the gospel to be so garbled, so muffled, or so freighted with language peculiar to religion that the average person hears it as some foreign tongue—abstract, remote, and strange. And that's too bad. For at its core the gospel says one thing and it says it with remarkable simplicity and clarity: Our misdeeds are not held against us; we are already forgiven (2 Cor. 5:18). It is the business of the church and its people to make that known.

Glen Edwards (*Broadmoor Baptist Bulletin,* Baton Rouge, LA.)

53
Knowing How and Where Not to Witness

Most of us have come to be pretty good experts on the subject of how and where not to witness for Christ. As modern, sophisticated, and sensible people, we have learned that certain methods of Christian witnessing are crude and obnoxious, and only turn people off rather than turn people to Christ.

Or at least that is what I keep thinking I have learned

until I continue to hear of persons who became a Christian because of some highly "unorthodox" method of presenting the good news to a non-Christian.

At a meeting of the Baptist World Alliance Committee on Religious Liberty and Human Rights, I heard a strange story set in Communist China. It reminded me once again that dignity and sophistication are not always the unshakable commandments for Christian witnessing. A distinguished musician in this officially antichristian country, the first violinist in the Peking National Symphony Orchestra, had a series of strange encounters with a man in the audience during several symphony concerts. At certain times during the concert the man in the audience would, without warning, slip quickly up to the stage and place a piece of paper in the hand of the first violinist, and then melt back into the crowd. The slip of paper had a Bible verse on it. This went on over a period of weeks, with nothing more nor less than this mysterious handing of notes to the musician, in each case a Bible verse.

Because of his acquaintance with then-Premier Chou En-lai, the violinist was able to leave the country and go to Hong Kong. He immediately went to Hong Kong Baptist College and asked if someone could direct him to a church where these Bible verses might be further explained and discussed. The distinguished violinist found his way into one of the Baptist churches in Hong Kong and it was not long before he had made a personal commitment to Christ as Savior. He has now dedicated that wonderful musical talent to Christian witnessing in his own special way.

It is stories like this one that help to remind me that I do not have all truth for all time in the matter of how to share the good news about the redeeming love of Christ. What might seem to be silly behavior to some, might simply be an innovative way to gain attention, in the minds of others. I still do not look with favor on grabbing a man by the lapels and asking "Are you saved, Brother?"

But who am I to say that God cannot accomplish a good result even in such a crude approach?

I have an idea our biggest problem in Christian witnessing in our day is that we spend far more time talking about how not to witness than we do talking about how to witness effectively. And the risks are not nearly so great as they are in Communist China.

Daniel R. Grant (*Arkansas Baptist Newsmagazine,* "One Layman's Opinion"), August 30, 1973, p. 2.

54
When You Drop the Hot Potato

I led a seminar on Christian witnessing at the recent state Baptist student convention which met at our church.

During the course of discussion I quoted Alan Richardson who once described the gospel as "hot potato news." Then I attempted to explain the quotation. I said, "Suppose you were out camping and had cooked your meal over an open fire. Someone reached in the coals and pulled out a potato wrapped in aluminum foil and tossed it to you. What would you do?" Very quickly a girl sitting on the front row said, "I would drop it."

She surely ruined that illustration! What I was driving at was that one doesn't just stand around holding a hot potato. One passes it on—or does something with it. But probably that girl's illustration was better than mine. That is what happens too much.

We have been given that kind of news: it is hot news; it is the kind of news that needs to be passed on. But what have we done? We have dropped it.

In *Tell It Like It Is* the young people sang:

It only takes a spark to get a fire going,
And soon all those around can warm up in its glowing;
That's how it is with God's love:
Once you've experienced it you spread his love to
  ev'ryone;
You want to pass it on.

I'll shout it from the mountaintop,
I want my world to know,
The Lord of love has come to me,
I want to pass it on.

So when you receive the good news, the "hot potato news," the gospel, don't just stand there and don't drop it. Pass it on.

PASS IT ON by Kurt Kaiser
© Copyright 1969 by LEXICON MUSIC   ASCAP
All rights reserved. International copyright secured.
Used by Special Permission.
James E. Carter, *People Parables* (Grand Rapids: Baker Book House), 1973, pp. 71-72.

───────────────────

55
A Tribute to My Father

My dad was not a Baptist preacher, but he was a very conscientious Baptist deacon.

As a Christian he took very seriously his responsibility to be a witness to Jesus Christ. I can remember one act of witness very well.

We had a next-door neighbor whom everyone called "Uncle Charlie." Uncle Charlie was a conductor on the KCS railroad. He was a good man. Everyone loved him. The children in the neighborhood were all crazy about him. But Uncle Charlie was not at that time a professing Christian.

One night my dad, Uncle Charlie, and I went to a high school football game. After the game we drove home, drove into our backyard where we stopped the car and parked under a sycamore tree. In that quiet, familiar setting Dad began to witness to Uncle Charlie.

He just simply told him what Christ had meant to him. He related how he had become a Christian; how it had changed his life completely; and how much he desired to see Uncle Charlie become a professing Christian and a church member.

There were no dramatics involved; no sermon; no high-pressure salesmanship; no threats nor dire warnings. It was just one concerned man sharing with a respected neighbor the love of God and the claim of Christ.

I have a lot of treasured memories of my father. I feel that my father left us a rich spiritual legacy. But this is one of my most treasured memories.

Personally, I think it is a tribute to a father that a son can remember him sharing his Christian faith with a friend. Can your children remember that?

56
When the Whole World Knows Your Secret

Once when I was very young I spent some time with my grandparents in Arkansas. Part of that time I spent with my mother's mother. Living on the farm adjoining hers was one of my mother's first cousins.

One day I was at his house. He was down in the pasture for some reason when he yelled back to the house for me to come quickly and to bring the .22 rifle with me. So down to the pasture I traveled with gun in hand and shells in pocket.

There was one lone tree in the middle of the pasture. In that tree was one lone squirrel. I was given the opportunity of killing that one squirrel in the tree. To tell the truth I don't remember how many shots I fired at that squirrel. I do remember, however, that it was more than one, several more than one. Then I hit him. That was the first squirrel I had ever killed.

Proud of my feat, I wrote home to tell my parents about it. That information was sent on a penny postcard.

Then about a day or two later, my father's oldest brother who worked in the post office in town called and inquired if I had seen the sheriff. When I told him I had not, he informed me that I probably would soon; the sheriff, he said, was after me for hunting out of season. That scared me, badly.

I spent several anxious days before someone ventured the opinion that my uncle had read the postcard in the post office and was playing a trick on me. While that was true, it taught me that there are some of your secrets you are not too interested in the whole world knowing.

But it also is true that we have few real secrets. After all, God knows. And things that you think may have been done totally secretly have a way of sneaking out. Also, what only one individual knows can through various ways and means become public knowledge.

On the other hand, there are some secrets that need to be shared with the whole world. Lovers are notorious about that. But what about the secret that you have found forgiveness in Christ; that you have peace of mind again; that through God's help you have gotten your head on straight and your life under control; that God has indeed become real to you? Share those secrets. Let the whole world know that secret. Who knows? Someone else may have been looking for the same secret.

PART III
Some Evangelistic Sayings

57
Definitions of Evangelism

Evangelism is a fellowship of reconciled and forgiven sinners feeling a personal responsibility and concern to make real to all men everywhere the reconciliation and forgiveness of God.

James S. Stewart, *The Wind of the Spirit* (New York and Nashville: Abingdon Press, 1968), p. 189.

The Church exists primarily for those who never go near it.

William Temple, quoted in Stewart, *The Wind of the Spirit* (New York and Nashville: Abingdon Press, 1968), p. 189.

The great apostle to the Islamic world, Sameral Zwemer, once wrote, "Evangelism is a collison of souls. We may measure its effect by an equation: $MV = i$ or mass $\times$ velocity $=$ impact."

Leighton Ford, *The Christian Persuader* (New York: Harper and Row, 1960), p. 11.

The church exists by mission as a fire exists by burning.
—Emil Brunner

But evangelism, in order to be true evangelism, must

157

cease to be a duty; it must become an inevitability. The shepherd looking for his last sheep is not fulfilling a duty; the mother praying for her erring child is not meeting an obligation; a church declaring God's judgments to the people is not just obeying a call; a friend sharing his friendship with Jesus is not simply discharging a responsibility.

D.T. Niles, "The Knock at Midnight," in *20 Centuries of Great Preaching*, Clyde E. Fant, Jr. and William M. Pinson, Jr. (Waco: Word Books, 1971), XII, p. 190.

The divine obligation of soul-winning rests without exception upon every child of God. The Christian receives the essence of this obligation and call at the time of his salvation. Regeneration demands reproduction in kind. The fruit of a Christian is another Christian. To witness for Christ is a spontaneous and natural expression of the newly saved child of God.

L.R. Scarborough, *With Christ After the Lost*, rev. E.D. Head (Nashville: Broadman Press, 1952), p. 2.

Evangelism is at the heart of all we do. It must be. Jesus said himself, "Joy shall be in heaven over one sinner that repenteth, more than over ninety and nine just persons, which need no repentance" (Luke 15:7). Evangelism makes heaven happy because it is the only hope—absolutely the only hope for sinful man.

Bailey E. Smith, *Real Evangelism* (Nashville: Broadman Press, 1978), pp. 152-153.

Evangelism is the outreach of the church by confrontation with the gospel of Christ, in an attempt to lead people to a personal commitment by faith and repentance in Christ as Savior and Lord.

C.E. Autrey, *The Theology of Evangelism* (Nashville: Broadman Press, 1966, pp. 13-14)

The evangelist is the man who believes that the gospel has an answer to man's deepest questions. He is like a man who has been freed from some evil habit, and he cannot keep from telling every other man in its grip the good news of how to be free. Personal witnessing is the power and strength of evangelistic preaching.

Gerald Kennedy, *The Seven Worlds of the Minister* (New York: Harper and Row, 1968), p. 142.

Christ's mission is the church's mission. As Jesus Christ came into the world to reveal God and to redeem men, the church is to serve as a channel of God's revelation and a proclaimer of redemption.

James E. Carter, *The Mission of the Church* (Nashville: Broadman Press, 1974), p. i.

D.T. Niles has defined evangelism as one beggar telling another beggar where to find bread.

58
One Beggar Telling Another

Until his retirement the late Wesley Lawton was a missionary in Taiwan. He had originally served as a missionary to China where his father had also been a missionary. Interestingly enough, the elder Lawton had five children, all of whom were missionaries.

Some years ago in a World Missions Conference, I heard Wesley Lawton tell the story about accompanying his father on a preaching trip when he was just a boy. As they left their home a beggar boy followed them to the railroad station. The elder Lawton told the boy they would be gone all day on a trip to another town but he would give him a copper coin if he would wait until he returned. With the promise of the copper coin he also told him to find other beggars and bring them, too. He would have a copper coin for each of them. The copper coins would buy each of them a bowl of soup.

When they returned they found two hundred beggars waiting for them at the railroad station! Then Lawton observed that after receiving the promise from his father the beggar boy was no longer a beggar but a missionary.

We have a promise from the Father. The beggar boy's promise from Wesley Lawton's father was for one copper coin for one day's soup. Our promise is for the forgiveness of sin and everlasting life.

That promise is backed up by the trustworthiness of God himself. We don't have to be concerned about whether it will be kept. The God who has given us life has also promised new life. God has proven himself trustworthy. His promises always stand. They are never broken.

Having the promises of God and knowing their trustworthiness our responsibility then becomes the responsibility of the beggar passing on the news. We have heard the good news. We have received forgiveness of sins. We have experienced the love of God. And that is not the kind of news we keep to ourselves. That is the kind of news we share with others.

We start spreading that news when we see ourselves as beggars. When we have come to realize that our salvation is not because of our goodness but of God's grace then we have the starting place. Perhaps some of us have been no more active in the sharing of where to find bread because we have not sufficiently realized our status as beggars before God.

With that sense of urgency we can soon spot others with

a similar need. And the beggars are all around us. They may live in luxury condominiums rather than slovenly hovels. They may ask, "How can I find a reason for living?" rather than, "What must I do to be saved?" They may have an empty, searching look in their eyes rather than the vacant, unnoticing stare of the starving. But beggars they are, as all of us once were, in the presence of God.

You start it right where you are—telling others where to find bread. Jesus healed a man once who wanted to go with him to tell the story but Jesus told him, "Go home to your friends, and tell them how much the Lord has done for you, and how he has had mercy on you" (Mark 5:19, RSV).

It is to the beggars around you that you tell where you found bread. The story has credibility then.

59
Using Language You Can Understand

My father-in-law had surgery on his back several years ago. The family, of course, was present at the hospital for the surgical procedure. It had lasted for several hours. I had wandered down the hall to talk to someone and was apart from the rest of the family when the surgeon came out to report to the family. As I came to the circle of the family surrounding the surgeon, my mother-in-law introduced me by saying, "This is my son-in-law, Dr. Carter." Immediately the surgeon turned from the rest of the family and began describing the procedure he had used to me in his best technical and medical terms. Of course, no one had explained to him that I wasn't that kind of doctor. We never did know what they had done to poor Granddaddy!

Our witness to Christ sometimes falls into that same trap. Using inside terms and technical theological language we never get around to explaining the love of God and the redemptive act of Jesus Christ in terms that common people can understand. What we have said may be theologically accurate, just practically obscure.

It is of no little significance that the Scripture records that the common people heard Jesus gladly. They heard him gladly because they could understand him and identify with what he said. Jesus was able to translate the most profound theological thought and insight into language that people could interpret.

The witness of Christ is not helped if people don't understand what is being said. While the word *saved* may mean something specific to the Christian, it may imply a practice of thrift to others. You are familiar, I am sure, with the way some people have changed the "Jesus Saves" signs by adding words to make it read "Jesus Saves Green Stamps." What Jesus saves is people; but it must be expressed clearly enough for people to understand it.

Someone has remarked that every profession is a conspiracy against the layman. By that they mean that every profession has an "inside" language, a group of busy words, a specialized vocabulary known only by the insiders. It would seem a conspiracy to keep the outsiders from knowing the secret. The very nature of Christianity is that it is not secret. It was not done in secret and is not propagated in secret. Christ died in a public execution. His people made public professions of faith in Him. The good news which is the gospel was designed to be shared.

We have something to report: God has provided salvation through Jesus Christ: His Son who died on the cross for us. Let us make sure that we give this report in language that people can understand, interpret, and apply to themselves.

60
The Test of Conversion

The test of a man's conversion is whether he has enough Christianity to get it over to other people. If he hasn't, there is something wrong in it. I could not do that. I began lay-reading when I was seventeen. I used to have a small summer congregation for whom I held services. Two or three men in that group met tragic experiences. Why? Partly because what I gave them was so general. There was no conversion in it. I could not get it across. I was like a Scotch friend of mine who said that while his friends could not make him drunk, he couldn't make them sober! There was a recurrent pattern of failure at those services, and working in army camps during the First World War. Individuals were seeking spiritual help, and I could not give it to them. Their faces still haunt me.

I went out to China to teach in a school in old Peking. Again, men were seeking. I should have failed them in the same way, but out there I met a man who challenged me as to whether I had ever made a full commitment of my life to Jesus Christ. He held me to it till I did it. And the very next day a Chinese businessman made his Christian decision with me. Test yourself by this: Can I get across to other people what I believe about Jesus Christ? If not, what real good am I to them, and what real good am I to Him?

Samuel M. Shoemaker, *How to Become a Christian* (New York: Harper and Row, 1953), p. 74.

61
The Importance of a Verbal Witness

I cannot, by being good, tell persons of Jesus' atoning death and resurrection, nor of my faith in His divinity. The emphasis is too much on me, and too little on Him. Our lives must be made as consistent as we can make them with our faith, but our faith, if we are Christians, is vastly greater than our lives. That is why the "word" of witness is so important. And that is why it is so important that the simplest of Christians know their faith, know some theology, and can give witness to what they believe about Jesus.

Sam Shoemaker, *Extraordinary Living for Ordinary Men* (Grand Rapids, Mich.: Zondervan Books, 1965), p. 117.

62
Our Evangelistic Task in This World

Our task becomes more and more the task of the early Christian missionary in the Roman Empire. We proclaim a way that has to be explained. We offer a gift that has to be defined. We shout out some good news that has to be justified. It becomes less practical to maintain ourselves by just warming up cold Christians or transferring church members from one church where they have had a bad experience to our church where they haven't had one yet but probably will in the future. This seems to me to say that evangelism has to be the center of the whole process once again if the church is to grow and society is not to be captured by some pagan way. And this is true not only for the fellow over in the vacant lot in a tent who is holding a two-week meeting, but for the cultured gentleman who fills the pulpit of the rich and traditional church on the avenue.

Gerald Kennedy, *The Seven Worlds of the Minister* (New York: Harper and Row, 1968), p. 127.

63
Nothing but the Gospel

"There is nothing better than the gospel," said a great man of God at thirty years of age, after examining the world philosophies. At forty, with the burdens of life on his shoulders, he observed: "There is nothing as good as the gospel." At fifty, with empty chairs in the family circle, he said: "Nothing can be compared with the gospel." At sixty, looking back on life with the realization that all would soon be over, he said: "There is nothing but the gospel."

Bob Woods, *The Challenger* (First Baptist Church, Muskogee, Okla., March 23, 1983), p. 2.

64
A Sense of Urgency

A textile salesman taught me a very valuable lesson. His name was Hans Samek, a Czechoslovakian refugee who came to the United States during World War II to sell top-quality British fabrics. I had met many good and great salesmen up to that time, but never had I seen a man show his line with such vigor, extol his products with such enthusiasm, or sell with such urgency. He approached every sale as if it were the last sale he'd ever make. His spirit was infectious, and before he was through, you wanted to buy as if it were the last chance you'd ever have to purchase such fine cloths. After one such session I turned to him and said, "Mr. Samek, you approach business with such a great sense of urgency. Do you brush your teeth with that same attitude?" "Why, of course," he replied, "I do brush my teeth urgently, as I do anything in life that's worth doing at all." I amended my grandmother's early advice of "Anything worth doing is worth doing well" by substituting the word "urgently" for "well."

This sense of urgency is a quality I search for in executives at all levels, and very infrequently find. The postwar years of continuing prosperity have made commercial life so relatively easy that few people have felt the necessity for an urgent approach to the solution for their business problems. When I discover a weakness in any of our stocks, I want to correct it today, not tomorrow, for in most cases the customer won't wait. When I learn of a dissatisfied customer, I try to establish personal contact immediately, having learned that the best adjustment is the quickest one. I'll telephone or pay a personal visit to straighten out a misunderstanding. If an employee has a grievance, I try to see the person before the store closes to prevent further aggravation overnight.

Stanley Marcus, *Minding the Store* (New York: Little, Brown and Co., 1974), pp. 171-172.

65
Forgetting the Purpose

We had just come out of the Greek Orthodox Church of the Annunciation in Nazareth. The church is built directly over Mary's well, the traditional place where the

angel appeared to Mary to announce the coming birth of
Jesus. It is fairly authentic since it is the only water source
in old Nazareth. It still has water. Once Turkish conquer-
ors rode their horses into the church to water them. After
that the water was piped out to a well on the street a little
way from the church.

The guide at the church was upset. After his explanation of the event and the place, we went to the altar, then
viewed the well through a grate. As we left, he asked for
tips and tried to sell slides and picture postcards. Since an
adequate tip had been given already for the group, individuals had been told there was no need to tip him
again. The slides did not sell well to our group either.
When we left, I saw the guide slam down his packages of
slides and utter angry words at us because we had not
been more profitable to him.

What a tragedy, I thought. *Here is a Christian and a
church who have entirely forgotten their purpose: to tell
the story of the birth of Jesus and its meaning to the
world. Here the preparation was made for the presence of
the Christ in the world. Now all energy and effort is put
into protecting a place whose purpose has been forgotten.*

James E. Carter, *Christ and the Crowds* (Nashville: Broadman Press, 1981), p.
7.

66
Losing the Opportunity

Ernest Gordon, dean of the chapel at Princeton University, tells that after the Christmas Eve service on the campus one year a rather shabbily dressed man made his way
through the crowd of worshipers and thrust a small paper
sack in his hand. In the sack were a book of poems and two

or three other possessions of such a nature that it was obvious they were the man's most cherished possessions.

But it was Christmas Eve. Students were shouting greetings to the chaplain. He was trying to return their greetings. In the press of the people and general excitement of the happy night the man who had brought the bag of gifts vanished, unidentified.

Two weeks later Gordon picked up the morning paper and saw the man's picture on an inside page. He had been struck and killed while walking along a highway. The encounter had been brief at best. The time for meeting, communication, sharing strength and help was neither offered nor taken. Any opportunity of helping that man was gone forever.

James E. Carter, *Christ and the Crowds* (Nashville: Broadman Press, 1981), p 34.

67
The Shame of Silence

One of the refreshing things about President Jimmy Carter was his forthright witness for Christ. In his book *Why Not The Best?*, he indicated that he had always joined the other deacons in the First Baptist Church of Plains, Georgia, in visiting the nonchurch families in their community prior to the annual revival.

One time he was invited to make a speech in a nearby church on the subject of "Christian Witnessing." As he worked on the message he thought he would add up the number of personal visits he had made for God. At that time he had been out of the Navy fourteen years. He had visited an average of two families a year. Assuming two parents and three children per family that would make a total of 140 visits. Proud of that, he wrote the figure in his notes.

The he remembered the 1966 campaign when he ran unsuccessfully for governor of Georgia. Since it was late when he decided to enter the campaign he determined to try to overcome the handicap. Leaving everything he cared for, he and his wife went in opposite directions shaking hands and trying to meet as many Georgia voters as possible. Working sixteen to eighteen hours a day at the end of the almost-successful campaign they had met more than 300,000 Georgians.

The comparison struck him. In three months he had made 300,000 visits for himself and 140 visits for Christ in fourteen years! Would you dare to make the same comparative figure? There is a shame to our silence in witnessing.

Jimmy Carter, *Why Not the Best?* (Nashville: Broadman Press, 1975), p. 133.

68
How We Prove the Love of God

In the novel *The Peaceable Kingdom,* Jan de Hartog tells the story of the men and women who began the Quaker movement in England. Approximately 100 years later they came to Philadelphia. One of the first to fall under the spell of George Fox, the founder of the Society of Friends, was Margaret Fell. In her new found love for God and man, she went into a prison near her home. The outrages she found there, especially toward children, were almost more than she could stand. Was there a God of love? If so, how could there be such pain and suffering? In her anger and frustration, she confronted George Fox: "Prove to me the existence of the God of love, or be condemned to hell for all the suffering thou hast caused me." George Fox sought to explain.

Margaret Fell would not listen. She badgered him relentlessly. Finally, he turned on her and said: "Stop crying for proof of God's love! Prove it thyself!" Then he added in a gentler tone: "How else dost thou think He can manifest His love? Through nature? Through the trees, the clouds, the beasts in the field, the stars? No, only through beings capable of doing so: ourselves. In the case of those children in the cage, about to be hanged, it is thou He touched. All He has to reach those children is thee!"

James E. Carter, *What Is to Come?* (Nashville: Broadman Press, 1975), pp. 72-73.

69
What Counts in Life

Sadie Virginia Smithson of Johnson Falls, West Virginia, grew up on the wrong side of town. She never found herself with the "in" group of her community. In desperation in the early 1900s she made a trip to Europe with money she had earned as a seamstress. She felt that out of this trip she would become a member of her community's literary league.

During the trip, World War I exploded across the Continent. One day Sadie Virginia Smithson found herself in the middle of a battlefield. After spending a day and night having last prayers with dying men, carrying water to the wounded, and writing fleeting letters home, Sadie found her entire value system reconstructed.

On the ship back home, one of her party said, "Well, Sadie, I guess you will now make the literary league."

"It don't matter no more," Sadie replied.

"Doesn't matter? What do you mean?" asked the questioner. Then Sadie related her story. "Well, Sadie, what does matter?" she asked.

Sadie replied, "Nothing except God, doing things for folks, and love."

James E. Carter, *Christ and the Crowds* (Nashville: Broadman Press, 1981), pp 96-97.

70
The Church of the Unsatisfied Shepherd

The spirit of the church should be that which Jesus described in the parable of the lost sheep—the unsatisfied heart of the shepherd. What a name for a church—the church of the unsatisfied shepherd!

G. Avery Lee, *What's Right with the Church?* (Nashville: Broadman Press, 19__), p 99.

. . .About the
Responsibility for Evangelism

71
Foundational

"The gospel is missionary. It's not information, it's good news. A congregation that's not missionary or evangelistic is denying its very basis for being."

Jimmy Draper, *Missions USA,* January/February, 1983.

72
The Specificity of God

The Bible's God always gets down to cases. He does not tell us to love all people; He commands us to love our neighbor, because our neighbor is a very specific person, right there on the spot. He does not ask us to show mercy in general; He points to the thirsty, the hungry, the imprisoned, the naked, and questions whether we have ministered to their very particular needs. He does not reveal Himself everywhere and always; He says, "This is my beloved Son . . . Listen to him." He does not ask for a general consensus of opinion about that Son; Jesus' question is, "But who do you say that I am?" Descriptions, commands, actions, decisions—these all have to do with specifics in the Bible, and if we would preach its good news, we also must learn to be that specific.

Elizabeth Achtemeir, *Creative Preaching* (Nashville: Abingdon Press, 1980), p 97.

73
Seeing Others Clearly

There is a great story about Joan Rivers, the humorist. She had been fitted for contact lenses. The first night she used them while performing she saw the audience for the first time in years. It was so frightening to her that she excused herself and took off her contacts and returned onstage to entertain a more familiar, faceless blur.

That's not unlike many of us spiritually. Our image of ourselves and others, as well as the magnificent beauty around us, is a dull blur, and often we would rather keep it that way. But if we want to see, really see with new vision, Jesus can heal us.

Lloyd John Ogilvie, *The Bush Is Still Burning* (Waco, Texas: Word Books, 1980), p. 80.

74
When God Is Near

I remember a story from the first book I ever read on the subject of prayer, A. J. Gordon's *Quiet Talks on Prayer*. It was about an occasion when the great evangelist, D. L. Moody, went to preach in a church in England. There was an iciness in the congregation, and Moody could not melt it. The preacher who had stirred hundreds of thousands of people in America felt leaden and stolid as he finished his sermon. The Spirit had not moved.

All afternoon Moody dreaded going back to preach

there again in the evening. It was a task he thought he could not endure.

But something happened in the evening service. It began with a look of warmth on a single face. Then it spread. Moody felt it surging like a tide, and, master preacher that he was, he rose on it, higher and higher. There was a great outpouring of the Spirit, and crowds of people streamed in the aisles after the sermon.

Later, they begged Moody to stay and preach for days; they knew revival was ready to break out. But he had to go on to Scotland and promised to come back again after his meeting there.

What had happened, he wondered, to change the atmosphere in that church between the morning and evening services? When he returned from Scotland he learned the answer.

Visiting in the home of an invalid church member, Moody discovered that she had read of his work and had been praying for months that God would send him to stir the smoldering coals of heartfelt religion in her church. The morning he had preached in the church, the woman's sister had come home and mentioned that an American named Moody had been the morning speaker. Astonished, the woman had wheeled herself into her room, saying she would have no lunch. All through the afternoon and into the evening, she had struggled with God over the issue of her church's deadness and its need for a revival.

That one woman, crippled and alone, Moody was convinced had been responsible for the dramatic change in the evening service. Singlehandedly, she had brought the Spirit into her church again.

John Killinger, *Bread for the Wilderness, Wine for the Journey* (Waco, Texas: Word Books, 1976), pp 91-93.

75
The Cruciality of Personal Contact

One of the more interesting periodicals to appear in 1978 was *Human Nature,* a monthly magazine devoted to the popularization of the behavioral sciences, such as social psychology and cultural anthropology. Because research in these complex areas tends to be rather technical and the jargon somewhat "heavy," the editors have shrewdly mixed their weighty studies with tidbits of lighter stuff sprinkled about under the caption "Common Knowledge." In a recent issue (August, 1978), I chanced to spot in the same collection (pp. 15-16) three unrelated entries, all of which made a strikingly similar point.

Let me begin by reprinting here these three squibs without further comment. As you read them, try to guess what feature I found them to share in common. Here is the first:

> Police received an alarm signal indicating a robbery was under way at the Mercantile and Industrial Bank.
>
> When a policeman telephoned the bank to check, one of the five bandits inside answered and calmly said it was a false alarm. They got away with $3,700.00.
>
> —United Press

Now for the second:

> A young Taiwanese man has written 700 love letters to his girl friend over the past two years trying to get her to marry him.
>
> His persistence finally brought results.
>
> A newspaper reported the girl has become engaged to the postman who faithfully delivered all the letters.
>
> —United Press

Finally, the third:

> Edmundo Nunez Merino, 59, respectfully raised his hat as a funeral cortege passed, little knowing that he was supposed to be in the coffin.
>
> He was spotted by his daughter as she accompanied what she thought was Merino's body to a cemetery in this southern Chilean city.
>
> She later explained to reporters that she had been told her father was dead when she went to visit him in a hospital. She made arrangements for the burial.
>
> Authorities were left with the task of identifying the body in the coffin.
>
> —Reuters

Probably you were tipped off by the title of this column regarding the unifying characteristic which I discovered in all three accounts. Notice that in every case, despite totally different circumstances, a crucial mistake was made by failure to establish firsthand contact. The policeman was content to telephone the bank, trusting any voice that answered to tell him what only a personal investigation could reveal. The Taiwanese man depended on love letters to express in writing what could adequately be conveyed only face-to-face. The daughter of Edmundo Nunez Merino took the word of a hospital offical that her father was dead but did not verify it with her own eyes.

As I smiled at these humorous yet serious episodes, suddenly I was struck by the realization that we make the very same mistake in much of our church work.

William E. Hull, "The Cruciality of Personal Contact" *Church Chimes* (First Baptist Church, Shreveport, Louisiana, January 25, 1979), p. 3.

76
Any Old Port in a Storm

I read about a woman who telephoned a friend and asked how she was feeling, "Terrible," came the reply over the wire, "my head's splitting and my back and legs are killing me . . . and the house is a mess, and the kids are simply driving me crazy." Very sympathically the caller said, "Listen, go and lie down. I'll come over right away and cook lunch for you, clean up the house, and take care of the children while you get some rest. By the way, how is Sam?"

"Sam?" the complaining housewife gasped. "I have no husband named Sam."

"My heavens," exclaimed the first woman, "I must have dialed the wrong number."

There was a long pause. "Are you still coming over?" the harried mother asked hopefully.

Bobby Moore, "Any Old Port in a Storm" (*First Baptist Informer,* First Baptist Church, Mineral Wells, Texas, May 13, 1981), p. 1.

77
Concern for Others

Perhaps you remember Conrad Richter's portrait of a praying minister in his novel *A Simple Honorable Man.* Harry Donner, a quiet, unpretentious pastor in a small coal-mining town in Pennsylvania, is such a good man that he continually overlooks his own welfare. When a large urban church offers him a fine salary and a postion of eminence, he prays about the call and decides to remain where he is because he thinks that is where God wants him to serve.

After Harry Donner dies, worn out from a life of selfless toil, his sons discuss how he used to groan at night, as if he were in great agony. One recalls the night the old man stayed with him and his wife: "It sounded like he was praying. You know how he used to break your heart sometimes when he prayed. When I was little, I never believed God could stand up to it."

Another son, determined to know more about this, calls on a woman in one of his father's former parishes and asks her about it. She says:

> Well, you come to the right place. We heard him a couple of years ago when he stayed with us on his way up to Tim's. He always liked to come here. After he went, Philip and I were talking. I told Philip it sounded to me like he was still doing in his sleep what he done all his life when he was awake, praying for them poor souls he'd seen ailing and suffering in this world. Mind you, he visited a lot of them. It sounded like he was begging God that this oughtn't to be and that oughtn't to be, and he had no right to let all them poor people under the harrow while folks like the Piatts rode rich and free.

John Killinger, *Bread for the Wilderness, Wine for the Journey* (Waco, Texas: Word Books, 1976), pp. 94-95.

78
Deliberately Disfiguring Oneself

In Eugene O'Neill's play *Days Without End,* Lucy Hill-
man says to Elsa Loving: "Yes, I went in for a little fleeting
adultery, and I must say, as a love substitute or even a
pleasurable diversion, it's greatly overrated. . . . You hit it
when you say disfigure. That's how I've felt ever since,
Cheap! Ugly! As if *I'd* deliberately *disfigured* myself."

Interpreter's Bible, George Arthur Buttrick, ed. (New York and Nashville: Abingdon Press), 1953, Vol. 2, p. 197.

The Three Hardest Words to Say

Somebody has well said that the three hardest words to
say like they ought to be said are these: "I have sinned."

George W. Truett, *A Quest for Souls* (Nashville: Broadman Press, 1945), p. 241.

The First Step to Grace

Someone tells of a man's first step to grace. As he was
shaving one morning he looked at his own face in the
mirror, and suddenly said, "You dirty, little rat!" And from
that day he began to be a changed man.

William Barclay, "The Gospel of Mark," *The Daily Study Bible* (Philadelphia:
The Westminister Press, 1954), p. 4.

79
The Menace of Mediocrity

H.G. Wells once wrote a fascinating story called "The Door in the Wall." It deals with a man who finally achieved great success and considerable acclaim who, as a small child, found his way through a door into a magnificently beautiful garden. While there, he was in another world. Walking about in the garden he felt a deep sense of peace and serenity. Then he had to leave.

As time passed he tried to find the door in the wall again, but never succeeded. However, as a grown man, he glimpsed the tiny door to the mystical garden on six occasions, but in each instance he had pressing engagements and did not have the time to enter the door.

On one occasion he was on his way to take the final exams which would lead to an Oxford career. Another time others were observing, and he was deterred by what they might think if he stopped to enter the mysterious garden. The other opportunities found him with pressing personal and professional demands which prevented him from going through the garden door: he was on his way to an important vote in the House of Commons, and at another time he was hurrying to visit his dying father. A final opportunity was passed up because he had a chance to become a cabinet member.

The things which deterred him were worthwhile, or at least understandable; but in each case the good became the enemy of the best. How often this is true of our church life and ministry. We pass by the little door that leads to fulfillment, peace, and purpose. We tend to forget that we can never attain the best unless we are willing to sacrifice some lesser good.

Bobby Moore, "The Menace of Mediocrity" (First Baptist *Informer,* ed. *Baptist Standard,* First Baptist Church, Mineral Wells, Texas, September 20, 1978), p. 1.

80
Accepting the Phony

So much of our world today is phony. Artist Tom Keating faked 3,000-year-old master paintings on the international market. He is a former house painter. He had worked for twenty-five years at fabricating Rembrandts, Goyas, Degases, and others. One of his forgeries sold for $42,000 (UPI, 8-28-76). This faking of old masters is a sophisticated means of robbery. It is also a testimony of how phony the world in which we live can become. People oohing over paintings that have been painted by a London house painter have lost the significance of what art really is.

Churches and Christians have a constant challenge to avoid counterfeiting the authentic moving of God in life. The path of counterfeiting is easily discernible. Few people do it crassly or purposefully. Most of the counterfeits in spiritual things come by overeagerness for the symptoms described in somebody else's spiritual pilgrimage. We work hard at duplicating them. Subconsciously we manage it. We try to make our experience with God identical with others, only to find that there are no two thumbprints alike. God does not create identical spiritual experiences. He does move in refreshing ways in people's lives.

Clifton R. Tennison, *The Baptist Visitor* (First Baptist Church, West Monroe, Louisiana, October 29, 1976), p. 1.

81
Importance of Conviction

The importance of this ministry of conviction was force-fully called to my attention one day as I stood in a public building in a great city. My eye was attracted to a poster with the promise of a huge reward for "information lead-ing to the arrest and conviction" of a certain fugitive from justice. This promise of reward was also accompanied by a picture and a detailed description of the wanted man. But frankly, the effect of the appeal was more monetary than personal. The sum of money involved was a tremen-dous amount, and the service rendered to the officers of the law was amazingly small—only a bit of information leading to the arrest and conviction of the criminal at large! It was then that the words, *"and conviction,"* stood out with sudden force. It is one thing to arrest a man; it is quite another thing to convict him, as any officer of the law can tell you. Indeed, as any preacher can tell you!

Ralph A. Herring, *God Being My Helper* (Nashville: Broadman Press, 1955), pp 85-86.

82
Hope Instead of Hell

John Wesley, the founder of the Methodist Church, hardly ever preached without describing the lost state of the human soul. The first part of his sermon was usually a description of a coming judgment on the sins of man-kind. He relates in his *Journal* an experience of his at Bath:

"I preached at Bath. Some of rich and great were present; to whom, as to the rest, I declared with all plainness of speech, 1. That, by nature, they were all children of wrath; 2. That all their natural tempers were corrupt and abominable; and 3. All their words and work,—which could never be any better but by faith; and that 4. A natural man has no more faith than a Devil, if so much. One of them, my Lord, stayed very patiently till I came to the middle of the fourth head; then starting up, he said, 'Tis hot!' 'Tis very hot,' and got down stairs as fast as he could."

John Henry Jowett, commenting on this entry, said that Lord So-and-So should have stayed until Wesley got to the marrow of his text, "The Son of Man is come to seek and to save that which was lost." For then he would have learned that over against the blackness of judgment there is the shining light of forgiveness.

Gerald Kennedy, *The Lion and the Lamb* (New York and Nashville: Abingdon Press, 1950, p 66.)

83
With God We Are Never Alone

Just before Easter, 1980, an elderly woman called the office of the Fort Worth (Texas) *Star-Telegram* from a hospital room. In a forty-five minute conversation with a reporter in the newspaper office, the woman revealed that she was eighty-one years old, that her husband and son were both dead, that she had no living relatives, and that she just wanted to tell someone good-bye before she died. After detailing her life, she indicated that she was not disillusioned or bitter about life; she just wanted to tell someone good-bye. She never did say who she was or where she was. She said good-bye. She was still alone, but she seemed satisfied.

The newspaper was swamped with calls the day the story about the woman was run. Older people, who were in similar situations, and younger people, who missed grandparents or who were separated from their parents, called wanting to know how to get in touch with the woman. They were willing to talk with her. They wanted to share her life and to help relieve her loneliness. With Christ in our world, we are never alone. At no time and at no place do we face life by ourselves. God is with us.

James E. Carter, *Christ and the Crowds* (Nashville: Broadman Press, 1981), pp. 11-12.

84
The Specificity of Love

I first met Joe Delaney when he was a high school student. He went to Haughton (Louisiana) High School where he played football and ran track. It was in connection with track that I met him. Our son Keith was also a runner. One of our high school classmates had a son who ran on the same relay teams as Joe Delaney. We would often see her at track meets and would sometimes sit with her. On one of those occasions she introduced us to Joe Delaney.

Then another of our high school classmates, A. L. Williams, who was the head football coach at Northwestern State University in Natchitoches, Louisiana, recruited Joe Delaney to play football at NSU. Before we left Natchitoches, we got to watch him play.

Joe did well in college football, so well that he was drafted by the Kansas City Chiefs. He really was scarcely big enough to play professional football. At five feet, ten inches in height and 184 pounds in weight he was overshadowed by many of the other players. But he was fast. He was quick. And he was remarkably agile. In 1981, as a rookie, he rushed for a team record of 1,121 yards and caught twenty-two passes. For that he was chosen Rookie of the Year.

The father of three children, Joe Delaney loved children. On a hot summer day in July, 1983, Joe Delaney was with some children in a park near Monroe, Louisiana. Two boys were swimming in a water hole that was formed when dirt was removed for a construction project. Delaney warned them not to swim in the twenty-foot hole; it was dangerous. But they swam there anyway. Hearing cries of distress, Joe Delaney dived into the pond to attempt to save the boys. Even though he could swim, Joe Delaney drowned in the rescue attempt. Both the boys drowned, too.

The Louisiana legislature was in session at the time. They passed a joint declaration of praise and appreciation for him. The NSU Homecoming had a special dedication and memorial in his honor. The memorial service was attended by many people including sports stalwarts from around the country.

Joe Delaney loved children. But he didn't just love children in general; he loved children in particular. In fact, he loved two children in particular so much that he gave his life in trying to save them.

God is that specific in His love for us. He loves each one of us specifically. Augustine observed that God loved each one of us as though there were only one of us to love. The fullness of God's love is experienced by each of us. That is a specific love.

And God asks us to love others specifically and not just generally. He wants us to love the child that disobeys the warning, the fellow worker who grates on the nerves, the neighbor that is hard to get along with, the friend that abuses the relationship.

The specificity of God's love delights us. The specificity of our love for others delights God. And Jesus reminded us, "Greater love hath no man than this, that a man lay down his life for his friends" (John 15:13). Love gets that specific.

85
A Summary of Theology

A minister friend of mine in Kentucky was present the night that Karl Barth spoke at Union Seminary in Richmond, Virginia. This was the only time the renowned Swiss theologian ever visited America, and after he had given a formal address he went down into the lounge to converse with the students. In the course of this exchange, a young man asked Dr. Barth if there were any way he could summarize the essence of what he had come to believe as a result of all his study. Barth unhurriedly reached into his pocket and got out his pipe, slowly filled it with tobacco, lit it, and for a moment disappeared in a cloud of smoke like Moses on Mount Sinai. Then as the smoke began to drift away, Barth said, "Yes, I think I can summarize my theology in these words: 'Jesus loves me, this I know, for the Bible tells me so.' "

My friend said he and his fellow students could hardly believe their ears. Here was the world's most eminent theologian reaching back for the simplest childhood hymn to express his faith. Yet, my friends, Barth was right —this is the essence of the gospel! Jesus loves me—what I am, where I am, when I am—and because He loves me, miracle of miracles, I can love myself. I can say yes to the name I have been given, to the event of my own creation and to what I have been, what I am, and what I can be. And this is what it means to be reconciled to God.

John Claypool, *The Light Within You* (Waco, Texas: Word Books, 1983), p. 216.

86
The Extravagance of Love

"The Gift of the Magi" by O. Henry is one of my favorite short stories. Della and Jim were a young couple who were very poor but very much in love. Each had one unique possession. Della's hair was her glory. When she let it down, it almost served as a robe. Jim had a gold watch, his pride, which had come to him from his father.

On the day before Christmas, Della had exactly one dollar eighty-seven cents with which to buy Jim a present. She did the only thing she could do: She went out and sold her hair for twenty dollars. With the proceeds, she bought a platinum fob for Jim's precious watch.

Jim came home from work that night. When he saw Della's shorn head, he stopped as if stupified. It was not that he did not like it or love her any more. She was lovelier than ever. Slowly he handed her his gift. His gift was a set of expensive tortoise-shell combs with jeweled edges for her lovely hair. He had sold his gold watch to buy them for her. Each had given all he or she had to give. Very clearly, love was extravagant in its actions.

James E. Carter, *Christ and the Crowds* (Nashville: Broadman Press, 1981), p. 91.

. . .About the
Savior

87
Jesus Christ:
The Theme of Preaching

If we are not determined that in every sermon Christ is to be preached, it were better that we should resign our commission forthwith and seek some other vocation. Alexander Whyte, describing his Saturday walks and talks with Marcus Dods, declared: "Whatever we started off with in our conversations, we soon made across country, somehow, to Jesus of Nazareth, to His death, and His resurrection, and His indwelling"; and unless our sermons make for the same goal, and arrive at the same mark, they are simply beating the air. It was a favorite dictum of the preachers of a bygone day that, just as from every village in Britain, there was a road to Christ. Possibly there were occasions when strange turns of exegesis and dubious allegorizing were pressed into service for the making of that road; but the instinct was entirely sound which declared that no preaching which failed to exalt Christ was worthy to be called Christian preaching. This is our great master theme.

James S. Stewart, *Heralds of God* (Grand Rapids, Mich.: Baker Book House, 1972), p. 61.

88
A Purpose in a Name

Jesus' purpose was in His name. The name *Jesus* is the Greek form of the Hebrew name *Joshua*. The name means "the salvation of God." When the name Jesus is repeated, the purpose of God is expressed: the salvation of God. Jesus was to come into the world to bring the salvation of God to people in need of salvation. What's in a name? Salvation is in that name.

James E. Carter, *Christ and the Crowds* (Nashville: Broadman Press, 1981), p. 11.

89
Christ's Presence Means Change

We don't really know how God will transform the lives of those who linger in his presence. Without a doubt, the lives of those shepherds were never the same again. In whatever manner God chooses to transform a life, He gives meaning to it. His presence means change.

Bruce Larson, in *The Edge of Adventure,* told of a men's group that was meeting one evening in an office in New York. A man came in whom no one knew. Each thought that he had been referred by someone else in the circle. They suggested he pull up a chair and join the six or eight men who were meeting for fellowship and prayer. The man sat and listened as several of the men talked about their present struggles toward becoming whole people and effective Christians.

Finally the leader turned to the stranger and asked who

he was. He replied by saying that his name was Paul and that as long as they were being honest, he would be honest, too. He was a dope addict. He had come there to rob the office to get a fix, but he thought he had found something better. Paul stayed to pray and asked God for help with his serious problem. He had come into the presence of Christ in the context of the very mundane setting of an office. But while there he had discovered that God was the source of any happiness he could have. The significance of that time spread out into eternity for him.

James E. Carter, *Christ and the Crowds* (Nashville: Broadman Press, 1981), p. 35.

90
No Subtle Cross

The president of Laukhuff Stained Glass Company of Memphis, Tennessee, was at the church to measure for the stained-glass windows which were to go over and on each side of the baptistry. While she and the pastor were waiting for the contractor to arrive, they discussed possible designs for the windows.

When they started talking about the two side windows she asked, "Would you object if I put a subtle cross in each of those windows?" She was assured that this would be fine.

What do you think about that? Do you have a subtle cross? How do you go about getting crucified subtly? When Jesus asked us to take up our cross and follow Him, did He mean for us to take up a subtle cross?

There was nothing subtle about the cross on which Christ died. It was set up on the "place of the skull" publicly. Everyone knew that a crucifixion was underway.

The place was so cosmopolitan that they had to write the sign in three languages.

Christ doesn't mean for us to take up a subtle cross either. He calls us to boldly declare ourselves to Him, to openly accept Him, and to actually surrender ourselves to Him.

A subtle cross would be a bloodless cross. And Christ would not allow that. A subtle cross would be a cross without commitment. There is no place in the Christian faith for that. A subtle cross would be a silent, secret cross. But faith demands open expression.

Too many of us have tried a subtle cross too long. Let's follow Christ's call and take up the cross of self-surrender and full commitment and follow Him—all the way.

91
Christ's Cross Changes Our Status

The cross establishes the worth of each human being regardless of whether he consciously stands before it. Consider this parallel. It is said that at the funeral procession of Abraham Lincoln a Negro mother lifted her child above the heads of the crowd and said, "Take a good look at that man. He died to set you free." That was true. What Lincoln had done during his presidency would affect that child, his children, and his children's children. By abolishing slavery Lincoln had radically and decisively changed the situation of all the future generations of Negroes in America.

In the same light the Bible sees the cross of Christ. God was on Golgotha. It was God's mighty act whereby He once and for all broke the enslaving power of evil that estranged us from Him, so that now we are free to go back to God and live as the obedient children of His love. The cross does more than lay a moral obligation on us. It

changes our status as human beings. It makes us persons
for whom Christ died.

Leonard Griffith, *The Need to Preach* (London: Hodder and Stoughton, 1971),
pp. 89-90.

92
No Provision for Defeat

During the Revolutionary War, General George Washington crossed the Brandywine with his army. After they
had crossed the bridge, his aide asked, "General, what
shall we do with the bridge?" Washington thought a
minute and said, "Burn it! Let us make no provision for
retreat. It is now victory or death!"

No provision was made for defeat.

With the resurrection of Jesus Christ from the dead no
provision was made for defeat. When Christ was crucified
it looked as though He had been defeated for good. But
He was not! There was no provision for defeat. Jesus rose
from the dead by the power of God.

Because of the resurrection the Christian does not have
to experience defeat. The power of God in Jesus Christ
enables the Christian to live in victory and power.

The reality of the resurrection does not reside simply in
the historical fact. Its reality is found in the living Lord
with whom Christians can have fellowship, guidance,
hope, and salvation. God doesn't expect us to be losers. He
expects us to be winners. By His power in Jesus Christ we
can be winners in life and in death.

Christ was not defeated by death. There was no provision for defeat. The Christian does not have to be defeated by sin nor by death. He draws His strength from the
power of God.

Paul expressed it this way:

For this corruptible must put on incorruption, and this mortal must put on immortality. So when this corruptible shall have put on incorruption, and this mortal shall have put on immortality, then shall be brought to pass the saying that is written, Death is swallowed up in victory. O death, where is thy sting? O grave, where is thy victory? The sting of death is sin; and the strength of sin is the law. But thanks be to God, which giveth us the victory through our Lord Jesus Christ (1 Cor. 15:53-57).

93
Christ Comes Through the Proclamation

From the English side of the Atlantic, I select Thomas Cook, an evangelist whose chief work was done in the last quarter of the nineteenth century and who, despite evangelistic tours in four continents, was little known outside his own church. Not even his friends claimed that, like Simpson, he had outstanding gifts. Indeed, it is astonishing how many people who sought to explain the power he could exert over a congregation began by saying, "He was such an ordinary person."

Thomas Cook was going to preach at a certain church over one weekend, and the friends who were to entertain him were so happy at the prospect of his coming that, long before the day arrived, they sickened the maid by the constant mention of his name. Collecting the meat at the butcher's on the Saturday morning, the irreverent girl mentioned the unnecessary fuss and said to the butcher, "You would think that Jesus Christ was coming!"

Thomas Cook came, and conquered the girl (as he had conquered thousands of others by the breath of God which seemed always to be about him), and when he appealed in the Sunday evening worship for an open avowal of discipleship from any who would make it, the maid came out.

Tuesday morning found her at the butcher's again, and the butcher, remembering her blasphemy three days before, asked the girl with a grin if Jesus Christ had come.

With awful earnestness she answered: "Yes. He came."

W.E. Sangster, *The Approach to Preaching* (Philadelphia: The Westminister Press, 1952), p. 27.

...About the
Eternal Destiny of the Person

94
Reason for Judgment

If God is righteous, He must exercise mercy on the obedient and mete out punishment to the disobedient. He would be as unrighteous if He left off judgment for the wicked as He would be if he left off blessings for the righteous.

Ray Summers, *The Life Beyond* (Nashville: Broadman Press, 1959), p 158.

95
Principles of Judgment

At the Greater Greensboro (North Carolina) Open Golf Tournament over the Easter weekend, 1972, South African golfer Gary Player failed to sign his scorecard after the third round and was disqualified. At that point, with only one round left to play, he was but one stroke behind the leader in the chase for the $40,000 first prize. By failing to sign his scorecard he was disqualified from the competition and did not win anything. In commenting on it afterward Player said, "There are rules in life, and we must abide by them." Someone then asked if there were not someone in the scoring tent to make sure that the cards were signed. To this Player replied, "My friend, there are responsibilities in life. You cannot shove your responsibilities onto the shoulders of someone else. This was my responsibility. I failed to meet it, so I must suffer the consequences."

Gary Player had voiced the reality of judgment.

Judgment is based on two principles: the responsibility of each person and the righteousness of God.

James E. Carter, *What Is to Come?* (Nashville: Broadman Press, 1975), pp. 91-92.

96
Face Christ as Defender or as Judge

When he was a young man, Judge Warren Candler practiced law. One of his clients was charged with murder, and the young lawyer made the utmost effort to clear his client of the charge. There were some extenuating circumstances, and the lawyer made the most of them in his plea before the jury. Moreover, there were in the court the aged father and mother of the man charged with murder; and the young lawyer worked on the sympathies and emotions of the jury by frequent references to the God-fearing parents.

In due course, the jury retired for deliberation. When they had reached a verdict, they returned to the jury box. Their verdict read: "We find the defendant not guilty." The young lawyer, himself a Christian, had a serious talk with his cleared client. He warned him to steer clear of evil ways and to trust God's power to keep him straight.

Years passed. Again the man was brought into court. Again the charge was murder. The lawyer who had defended him at his first trial was now the judge on the bench. At the conclusion of the trial, the jury rendered its verdict—"Guilty."

Ordering the condemned man to stand for sentencing,

Judge Candler said, "At your first trial, I was your lawyer; today I am your judge. The verdict of the jury makes it mandatory for me to sentence you to be hanged by the neck until you are dead."

Billy Graham, *World Aflame* (New York: Doubleday, Pocket Cardinal Edition, 1966), p. 208.

97
How to Preach About Hell

We cannot contemplate hell without a note of sadness. Anyone who derives pleasure from the thought of hell has something wrong. Perhaps you have heard the description of the two preachers. One of them preached about hell as though he were glad of it. The other preached about hell with a sob in his voice. And we cannot but sob when we realize that this is the eternal destiny of some people.

James E. Carter, *What Is to Come?* (Nashville: Broadman Press, 1975), p. 130.

98
The Meaning of Hell

We were driving just outside of the old walled city of Jerusalem when the tour guide said over the loud speaker: "We are now in the valley of Hinnom." I turned to my wife and said: "You are now right in the middle of hell."

Our English word *hell* translates a word that means the valley of Hinnom. The valley of Hinnom was immediately southeast of the city of Jerusalem. In ancient times it had been the location of the worship of the heathen god Molech, which included burning babies alive. This practice was abolished by King Josiah, and the place came to be used by the Jewish people as a place for garbage disposal, including the refuse from the city, the bodies of animals, and even the bodies of criminals who had no one to give them burial. A fire was kept going continuously for sanitary purposes. The term came to be generally used to present the idea of that which is abominable.

James E. Carter, *What Is to Come?* (Nashville: Broadman Press, 1975), pp. 119-120.

99
What Do You Want God to Do?

In the long run, the answer to all those who object to the doctrine of hell, is itself a question: "What are you asking God to do?" To wipe out their past sins and, at all costs, to give them a fresh start, smoothing every difficulty and offering every miraculous help? But He has done so—on Calvary. To forgive them? They will not be forgiven. To leave them alone? Alas, that is what He does.

C. S. Lewis, *The Problem of Pain* (London: Fontana Books, 1957), p. 116.

100
The Symbols of Hell

The conditions in hell have always interested people. The Bible speaks in symbols. Don't dismiss the idea of hell because you can't answer the question of how there is eternal fire with flames that illumine and outer darkness at the same time. The figures used to describe hell all speak of pain, separation, anguish, grief, and alienation. You don't have to push them to extremes in order to accept the biblical teachings about hell.

This has often been fertile ground for people with active imaginations. In fact, many of the ideas about hell have come from amplifications of the scriptural symbols. Harry Emerson Fosdick wrote in his autobiography that as a child he had nightmares about hell from some of the sermons that he heard describing its horrors. But hell is real, even though some people have pushed the symbols beyond their intended limits.

An extremely conservative church was located about two blocks from the elementary school I attended as a boy. To advertise their church and to warn against the danger of delay in accepting Christ, the church had erected a large billboard next to the sidewalk and running parallel to the church auditorium. In brilliant colors a raging fire was painted. Suspended over the fire was a man in a prone position. Lettered on the sign were appropriate words of warning. I don't know how many people that sign turned to Christ. But I can imagine the deep impression that it must have made on the minds of school-children as they passed the sign day after day.

James E. Carter, *What Is to Come?* (Nashville: Broadman Press, 1975), pp. 124-125.

101
Heaven: Where the Road with God Leads

We are afraid that heaven is a bribe and that if we make it our goal we shall no longer be disinterested. It is not so. Heaven offers nothing that a mercenary soul can desire. It is safe to tell the pure in heart that they shall see God, for only the pure in heart want to. There are rewards that do not sully motives.

C. S. Lewis, *The Problem of Pain* (London: Fontana Books, 1957), p. 133.

A man with sin in his heart could not be happy anywhere in God's universe; he would convert any paradise into a hell. Character is more than environment.

W. T. Conner, *Christian Doctrine* (Nashville: Broadman Press, 1937), pp. 321-22.

Heaven is not a cash payment for walking with God; it is where the road leads.

Austin Farrar in James E. Carter, *What Is to Come?* (Nashville: Broadman Press, 1975), p. 106.

102
Our Hope of Heaven

The late M. E. Dodd, longtime pastor of First Baptist Church, Shreveport, Louisiana, told the following story:

A son of a Baptist preacher drifted away from God when his father died, though he had shared family devotions, Bible study, and church attendance during the father's lifetime. He collapsed when, some years later, his mother died.

Dodd sent the son a telegram: "Love, prayers, and sympathy. Read First Thessalonians four thirteen eighteen." The son read the telegram perfunctorily and set it aside. After the funeral, however, as he was going through messages from friends, he came upon Dodd's telegram. Picking up his mother's Bible, he turned to the reference and